JAMESTOWN EDUCATION

Reading Science

Strategies for English Language Learners

High Intermediate

McGraw Hill Glencoe

New York, New York   Columbus, Ohio   Chicago, Illinois   Peoria, Illinois   Woodland Hills, California

JAMESTOWN EDUCATION

Image Credits: Cover (prism)ThinkStock, (satellite)CORBIS,
(globe)Creatas, (others)Getty Images.

 **Glencoe**

The *McGraw·Hill* Companies

Send all inquiries to:
Glencoe/McGraw-Hill
8787 Orion Place
Columbus, OH 43240-4027

ISBN 0-07-872916-5 (Student Edition)
ISBN 0-07-874226-9 (Teacher Edition)

Printed in the United States of America.

2 3 4 5 6 7 8 9 10 066 11 10 09 08

Contents

To the Student

Reading is one of the fastest ways for you to get information. *Reading Science* can help you improve the way you read and understand science topics. You will also learn how to improve your test-taking skills.

Before You Read

These steps can help you *preview* an article and get an idea of what it is about.

Read the title. Ask yourself "What can I learn from the title?" and "What do I already know about this subject?"

Read the first sentence or two. The writer wants to catch your attention in the first sentence or two. You may also find out what you are about to learn.

Skim the entire article. Look over the article quickly for words that may help you understand it. Jot down unfamiliar words in your Personal Dictionary. You can ask someone later what they mean.

Participate in class discussions. Your teacher may show you pictures or objects and ask you questions about them. Try to answer the questions.

While You Read

Here are some tips to help you make sense of what you read:

Concentrate. If your mind wanders, remind yourself of what you learned when you previewed the article.

Ask yourself questions. Ask yourself "What does this mean?" or "How can I use this information?"

Look for the topic of each paragraph. Each paragraph has a main idea. The other sentences build on that idea. Find all of the main ideas to understand the entire article.

Refer to the vocabulary you have learned. The words in dark type will remind you of what you learned in the Vocabulary section. For more help, refer to the previous page.

After You Read

The activities in *Reading Science* will help you practice different ways to learn.

A. Organizing Ideas Webs, charts, and tables will help you organize information from the article. Sometimes you will create your own art.

B. Comprehension Skills will help you recall facts and understand ideas.

C. Reading Strategies will suggest ways to make sense of what you read.

D. Expanding Vocabulary will teach you more about the vocabulary you learned before and during reading.

Vocabulary Assessment

After every five lessons, you can try out what you have learned. Activities, such as postcards and advertisements, show you how the vocabulary can be useful and fun in everyday life. Enjoy!

Pronunciation Key

a	as in *an* or *cat*	**k**	as in *kitchen, book, mock,* or *cool*
ä	as in *father* or *arm*	**l**	as in *look, alive, heel, tall,* or *follow*
ā	as in *made, say,* or *maid*	**m**	as in *me, imagine,* or *seem*
e	as in *wet* or *sell*	**n**	as in *no, inside, inning,* or *fun*
ē	as in *he, see, mean, niece,* or *lovely*	**ng**	as in *singer, bring,* or *drink*
i	as in *in* or *fit*	**p**	as in *put, open,* or *drop*
ī	as in *I, mine, sigh, die,* or *my*	**r**	as in *run, form,* or *wear*
o	as in *on* or *not*	**s**	as in *socks, herself,* or *miss*
ō	as in *fold, boat, own,* or *foe*	**sh**	as in *should, washing,* or *hash*
ô	as in *or, oar, naughty, awe,* or *ball*	**t**	as in *too, enter, mitten,* or *sit*
oo	as in *good, would,* or *put*	**th**	as in *think, nothing,* or *tooth*
o̅o̅	as in *roof* or *blue*	**t͟h**	as in *there, either,* or *smooth*
oi	as in *noise* or *joy*	**v**	as in *vote, even,* or *love*
ou	as in *loud* or *now*	**w**	as in *well* or *away*
u	as in *must* or *cover*	**y**	as in *yellow* or *canyon*
ū	as in *pure, cue, few,* or *feud*	**z**	as in *zoo, hazy,* or *sizes*
ur	as in *turn, fern, heard, bird,* or *word*	**zh**	as in *seizure, measure,* or *mirage*
ə	as in *awhile, model, second,* or *column*	**N**	as in *bonjour* (vowel before the **N** is nasal)
f	as in *fat, before, beef, stuff, graph,* or *rough*	**KH**	as in *loch* (or German *ach*)
g	as in *give, again,* or *dog*		
h	as in *hat, whole,* or *ahead*		

Our Solar System

Before You Read

 **Think about what you know.** Read the lesson title above. What do you predict the article will be about? What do you know about our solar system?

Vocabulary

The content-area and academic English words below appear in "Our Solar System." Read the definitions and the example sentences.

Content-Area Words

gravity (grav′ə tē) the force that pulls objects toward a star or planet, such as Earth
> *Example:* *Gravity* keeps us from floating off the ground.

universe (ū′nə vurs′) everything that exists in space, including stars and planets
> *Example:* The planets, the Moon, and the stars are all part of the *universe*.

astronomers (əs tron′ə mərz) people who study the science of the planets and stars
> *Example:* The *astronomers* discovered new stars after studying the sky for years.

fusion (fū′zhən) the process of using great heat to combine elements
> *Example:* An experiment that uses *fusion* will create great energy.

glowing (glō′ing) shining; letting off light and sometimes heat
> *Example:* A little *glowing* lamp was the only light in the room.

Academic English

comprises (kəm prīz′əz) is made of or includes
> *Example:* A milkshake *comprises* milk, ice cream, and sometimes chocolate syrup.

survive (sər vīv′) to remain alive
> *Example:* The lost campers were able to *survive* in the cold weather until they were rescued.

Do any of the words above seem related? Sort the seven vocabulary words into two or more categories. Write the words down on note cards or in a chart. Words may fit into more than one group. You may wish to work with a partner for this activity.

Dictionary Now skim the article and look for other words that are new to you. Write each new word and its definition in the Personal Dictionary.

While You Read

Tip! **Think about why you read.** Have you ever seen a drawing of our solar system on a poster or in a book? As you read, look for information about the objects in our solar system.

Our Solar System

1 A solar system is made up of a star, the planets that orbit (or circle) it, and everything else that is held in by the **gravity** of the star. Our solar system is made up of the Sun, the planets, and millions of smaller objects, such as asteroids, comets, and meteoroids. Our solar system is one of many solar systems in the
5 **universe. Astronomers** have found at least fifty other solar systems so far.

The Sun **comprises** only gases. Gas, such as air, is matter that has no shape. The middle, or core, of the Sun contains hydrogen gas, which comes from the chemical hydrogen. Hydrogen goes through **fusion** to make a different kind of gas, called helium. Fusion gives off heat and light energy. This energy is so
10 powerful that the core of the Sun has a temperature of about 15 million degrees Celsius (27 million degrees Fahrenheit). Everything that lives on Earth needs the heat and light of the Sun in order to **survive.**

In our solar system, Mercury, Venus, Earth, and Mars are the inner planets. They are the closest planets to the Sun. They are a group of rocky planets. The
15 inner planets are surrounded, or circled, by a large ring of asteroids, called an asteroid belt. Jupiter, Saturn, Uranus, and Neptune are the outer planets. They are farther away from the Sun. They probably do not have solid surfaces. They have thick outer layers of gas. Thin rings of dust, rock, and ice surround each of the outer planets. Most of the planets have at least one moon.

20 Pluto is the planet farthest from the Sun. Pluto is a tiny, solid planet with a strange orbit. The path it makes around the Sun is not like the paths of the other planets. Most astronomers do not think of Pluto as a very important planet.

Many smaller objects orbit the Sun. Asteroids are the largest of these objects. Most asteroids are found in the asteroid belt between Mars and Jupiter. The largest
25 known asteroid, Ceres, is about 925 kilometers (575 miles) across.

Comets are made of ice and rock. Comets come from the coldest parts of our solar system. Objects in this part of the solar system are sometimes pushed into new orbits. As a comet gets close to the Sun, the ice in its core turns to gas. It leaves a trail of **glowing** dust and gases behind it, called a tail.

30 The other objects in our solar system break off from asteroids, comets, and moons. These broken chunks of rock and metal are called meteoroids. Sometimes one of these space rocks lands on Earth. When this happens, it reminds us that there are other objects in our solar system.

CONTENT CONNECTION

The planets are listed in order of their closeness to the Sun. The temperature on Mercury is very hot. Why do you think it is so hot?

LANGUAGE CONNECTION

Living things such as dogs and lizards have tails. A comet is not alive but has a tail. What are the tails of other things made of? Kites? Airplanes? Ponytails?

After You Read

A. Organizing Ideas

What objects are in our solar system? Complete the triangle chart below. Write the names of the smallest objects in our solar system at the bottom of the triangle. Write the names of the planets in the middle of the triangle. Write the name of the largest object in our solar system at the top of the triangle. Some have been done for you.

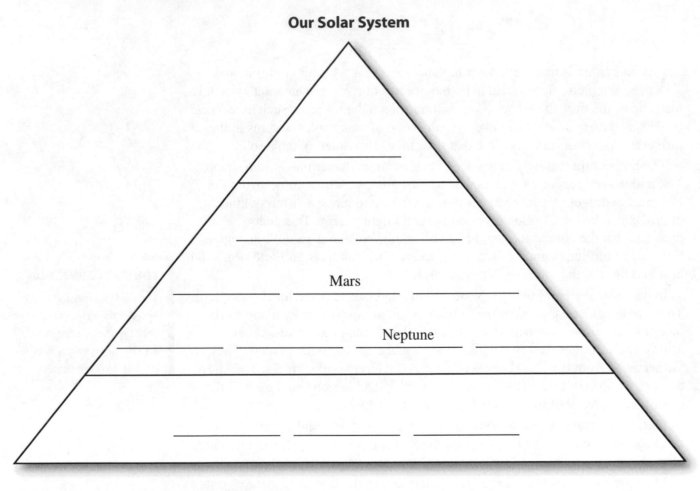

Our Solar System

Mars

Neptune

What did you learn about the parts of our solar system by completing this chart? Write two or more sentences about what the shape of this chart tells you about the objects in our solar system. How was this chart a helpful learning tool for you? Explain your answer.

_____

_____

_____

_____

B. Comprehension Skills

 Think about how to find answers. Look back at what you read. The information is in the text, but you may have to look in several sentences to find it.

Mark box **a, b,** or **c** with an **X** before the choice that best completes each sentence.

Recalling Facts

1. Jupiter is a
   - ☐ **a.** moon.
   - ☐ **b.** planet with a thick outer layer of gas.
   - ☐ **c.** rocky planet that is close to the Sun.

2. The star at the center of our solar system is
   - ☐ **a.** Pluto.
   - ☐ **b.** Ceres.
   - ☐ **c.** the Sun.

3. Meteoroids are
   - ☐ **a.** stars.
   - ☐ **b.** liquid planets.
   - ☐ **c.** pieces of rock and metal.

4. A solid planet with a strange orbit around the Sun is
   - ☐ **a.** Pluto.
   - ☐ **b.** Uranus.
   - ☐ **c.** Neptune.

5. We call a star, along with the planets and smaller objects that orbit it,
   - ☐ **a.** a comet.
   - ☐ **b.** helium gas.
   - ☐ **c.** a solar system.

Understanding Ideas

1. Astronomers do not group Pluto with the other planets because it is
   - ☐ **a.** a star.
   - ☐ **b.** close to the Sun.
   - ☐ **c.** very different from the other planets.

2. From the article, you can conclude that planets are found
   - ☐ **a.** only in our solar system.
   - ☐ **b.** outside our solar system.
   - ☐ **c.** only within the asteroid belt.

3. At the very center of a solar system is a
   - ☐ **a.** star.
   - ☐ **b.** comet.
   - ☐ **c.** planet.

4. From the article, you can conclude that all large and small objects in a solar system orbit
   - ☐ **a.** a star.
   - ☐ **b.** a moon.
   - ☐ **c.** the largest planet.

5. You can also conclude that as a comet moves away from the Sun,
   - ☐ **a.** it collides with a planet.
   - ☐ **b.** it leaves the solar system.
   - ☐ **c.** its gases change back to ice.

C. Reading Strategies

1. Recognizing Words in Context

Find the word *solid* in the article. One definition below is closest to the meaning of that word. One definition has the opposite or nearly the opposite meaning. The remaining definition has a meaning that has nothing to do with the other two words. Label the definitions **C** for *closest*, **O** for *opposite* or *nearly opposite*, and **U** for *unrelated*.

_____ **a.** hollow

_____ **b.** filled

_____ **c.** round

2. Distinguishing Fact from Opinion

Two of the statements below present *facts*, which can be proved. The other statement is an *opinion*, which expresses someone's thoughts or beliefs. Label the statements **F** for *fact* and **O** for *opinion*.

_____ **a.** Pluto is the planet farthest from the Sun.

_____ **b.** Astronomers like to study Venus more than Mars.

_____ **c.** Sometimes meteoroids land on Earth.

3. Making Correct Inferences

Two of the statements below are correct *inferences*, or reasonable guesses, that are based on information in the article. The other statement is an incorrect, or faulty, inference. Label the statements **C** for *correct* inference and **I** for *incorrect* inference.

_____ **a.** Plants, animals, and people on Earth need the Sun to stay alive.

_____ **b.** Pluto is probably the darkest, coldest planet.

_____ **c.** Comets are dangerous to life on Earth.

4. Understanding Main Ideas

One of the statements below expresses the main idea of the article. Another statement is too general, or too broad. The other explains only part of the article; it is too narrow. Label the statements **M** for *main idea*, **B** for *too broad*, and **N** for *too narrow*.

_____ **a.** Mercury, Venus, Earth, and Mars are rocky planets, and they are closest to the Sun.

_____ **b.** There are many solar systems in the universe, and ours is one of them.

_____ **c.** Our solar system is made up of the Sun, as well as the planets, asteroids, comets, and meteoroids that orbit it.

5. Responding to the Article

Complete the following sentences in your own words:

After reading "Our Solar System," I would like to learn more about

_____

I could learn more by _____

_____

D. Expanding Vocabulary

Content-Area Words

Cross out one word or phrase in each row that is not related to the word in dark type.

1. gravity	pull	force	downward	float
2. universe	empty	everything	Earth	space
3. astronomers	water	stars	scientists	planets
4. fusion	atoms	hot	separate	energy
5. glowing	shining	bright	dark	comet

Academic English

In the article "Our Solar System," you learned that *comprises* means "is made of or includes." *Comprises* can express how the Sun is made up of gases. *Comprises* can also express what other things are made up of, as in the following sentence.

Lemonade comprises water, lemon juice, and sugar.

Complete the sentence below.

1. The book *comprises* an introduction, a table of contents, and _____

Now use the word *comprises* in a sentence of your own.

2. _____

_____

You also learned that *survive* means "to remain alive." *Survive* can also mean "to live after another person's death," as in the following sentence.

Three sons survive their mother.

Complete the sentence below.

3. Now that she is sick, she may not *survive* her _____

Now use the word *survive* in two sentences of your own.

4. _____

5. _____

 Share your new sentences with a partner.

A Journey Through the Eye

Before You Read

 Think about what you know. Read the lesson title above. What do you predict the article will be about? What do you know about how our eyes work?

Vocabulary

The content-area and academic English words below appear in "A Journey Through the Eye." Read the definitions and the example sentences.

Content-Area Words

organ (ôr´gən) a part of the body that does a specific task or job
Example: The heart is an *organ* that pumps blood through the body.

muscles (mus´əlz) tissues in the body that work together to move parts of the body
Example: You use the *muscles* in your arms to reach, touch, and hold things.

focuses (fō´kəs iz) aims something at a certain point
Example: A runner *focuses* her eyes on the finish line of the race.

nerve (nurv) a tiny, ropelike band of tissue that carries signals between the brain, spinal cord, and other parts of the body
Example: *Nerves* in my toes warned me that the water was cold.

pigment (pig´mənt) something that gives color
Example: The artist used yellow *pigment* to make the paint yellow.

Academic English

images (im´ij əz) the mind's pictures of things
Example: I can still see *images* of trees and water from my trip to the lake.

adapt (ə dapt´) to change in order to become used to different conditions
Example: The dog will *adapt* to living indoors instead of outdoors.

Answer the questions below. Circle the part of each question that is the answer. The first one has been done for you.

1. If an animal *adapts* to cold weather, does it stay the same or change?
2. Are *nerves* more like messengers or teachers?
3. Does an *organ* make the body look good or do work?
4. Are *images* made in the brain or in the heart?
5. Would a frog that *focuses* his sight on an insect watch it carefully or ignore it?
6. Which has *pigment* in it, a red drink bottle or a clear glass window?
7. Do you use your *muscles* to think about your grandmother or to dance?

Dictionary Now skim the article and look for other words that are new to you. Write each new word and its definition in the Personal Dictionary.

While You Read

Tip! **Think about why you read.** When you enter a dark room, what happens to the way you see? As you read, look for information that tells you why this happens.

A Journey Through the Eye

1 The human eye works together with the brain to help us see. Thin lines of light, called rays, bounce off objects and travel through the eye. The eyes let in the light and send signals, or messages, to the brain. These signals create the pictures, or **images,** that we see.

5 The eye is a round **organ** filled with clear liquid. When light goes into the eye, it first passes through the cornea. The cornea is a clear layer on the outside of the eyeball. It helps keep the eye safe and moves light deep into the eye.

Next, light travels through the pupil. The pupil is a black spot that controls how much light enters the eye. Around the pupil is the round, colorful iris. The
10 **muscles** of the iris relax and become looser to open the pupil. When you try to see in a dark or dim room, the pupil opens to let more light in. In a very bright room, the iris becomes tighter to make the pupil smaller. Less light goes into the eye when the pupil is smaller.

From the pupil, light travels through a clear circular disk called a lens. The
15 lens **focuses** light and can change its shape to focus on objects that are at different distances. The lens bulges, or curves outward, to focus on objects that are close by. It flattens out to focus on objects that are far away.

Focused light from the lens hits the retina, which is on the back of the eyeball. The retina is made up of **nerve** cells called rods and cones. The rods help us see
20 in black and white when we are in the dark. The cones help us see colors when we are in brighter light. When a person enters a dark room after being in bright light, his or her eyes have to **adapt** to the change. The pupil grows wider to let in as much light as possible. This helps the person see in the dark. But changes in the pupil are not enough to help us see when light changes quickly to dark. The retina
25 helps too. A **pigment** in the rods makes it possible for us to see in the dark. Bright light bleaches this pigment, or turns it white, and stops it from working. It takes time for the pigment to come back so that the eyes can see in the dark.

As light hits the rods and cones, the retina sends messages to the brain. The messages travel along a nerve called the optic nerve. Different parts of the brain
30 work together to understand the messages from the eyes, and then an image is formed. With messages from both eyes, the brain can understand the size, movement, distance, and speed of the objects you see.

CONTENT CONNECTION

The lenses in your eyes help you focus on objects that are both close and far away. Glasses and contact lenses can adjust focus. What else can they do?

LANGUAGE CONNECTION

Notice the word *bleaches*. People use a chemical called bleach to make white clothes brighter. What may happen if you bleach colored clothes?

After You Read

A. Organizing Ideas

What do you know or want to know about the way your eyes work? Complete the K-W-L chart below. List four things you know, four things you want to learn about, and four facts you have learned from the article about how the eye works. Some of the items have been done for you.

What I Know	What I Want to Know	What I Have Learned
Part of my eye is called the pupil.		The pupil is the black spot in the middle of my eye. Its job is to control the amount of light that goes into my eye. It opens and closes to do its job.
		A pigment in the rods helps the eyes see in the dark. It takes time for the pigment to come back.
I can see things that are both close and far away.	How can the eyes focus on things that are both close and far away?	

Did you learn more about something that you already knew as you completed this chart? Write two or more sentences about something new that you have learned about the way your eyes work. What other way could you organize this material?

_____

_____

_____

_____

_____

B. Comprehension Skills

Tip! **Think about how to find answers.** Think about what each sentence means. Try to say it to yourself in your own words before you complete it.

Mark box **a, b,** or **c** with an **X** before the choice that best completes each sentence.

Recalling Facts

1. The retina is made up of
   - ☐ **a.** lenses.
   - ☐ **b.** clear liquid.
   - ☐ **c.** cones and rods.

2. The eye is a
   - ☐ **a.** thin disk.
   - ☐ **b.** solid ball.
   - ☐ **c.** ball filled with liquid.

3. Messages travel to the brain along
   - ☐ **a.** a bone.
   - ☐ **b.** a nerve.
   - ☐ **c.** a blood vessel.

4. The part of the eye that can change shape to focus on objects at different distances is
   - ☐ **a.** the lens.
   - ☐ **b.** the pupil.
   - ☐ **c.** the retina.

5. The parts of the body that help us see are the eyes and
   - ☐ **a.** the ears.
   - ☐ **b.** the brain.
   - ☐ **c.** the rest of the face.

Understanding Ideas

1. Light travels through the cornea and lens before it
   - ☐ **a.** hits the retina.
   - ☐ **b.** reaches the eye.
   - ☐ **c.** passes through the pupil.

2. From the article, you can conclude that it would be impossible to see without any
   - ☐ **a.** light.
   - ☐ **b.** cones.
   - ☐ **c.** pigment.

3. The parts of the eye that adjust to quick changes in lighting are
   - ☐ **a.** the pupil and the retina.
   - ☐ **b.** the lens and the nerve cells.
   - ☐ **c.** the cornea and the optic nerve.

4. In bright sunlight, the pupil probably
   - ☐ **a.** opens to let in all light.
   - ☐ **b.** closes a bit to keep out some light.
   - ☐ **c.** closes to keep out all light.

5. From the article, you can conclude that the signals that travel to the brain along the optic nerve are based on changes in
   - ☐ **a.** the lens and the cornea.
   - ☐ **b.** the liquid that fills the eye.
   - ☐ **c.** the shape of the light that hits the retina.

C. Reading Strategies

1. Recognizing Words in Context

Find the word *travels* in the article. One definition below is closest to the meaning of that word. One definition has the opposite or nearly the opposite meaning. The remaining definition has a meaning that has nothing to do with the other two words. Label the definitions **C** for *closest*, **O** for *opposite* or *nearly opposite*, and **U** for *unrelated*.

_____ **a.** speaks loudly

_____ **b.** stays still

_____ **c.** moves

2. Distinguishing Fact from Opinion

Two of the statements below present *facts,* which can be proved. The other statement is an *opinion,* which expresses someone's thoughts or beliefs. Label the statements **F** for *fact* and **O** for *opinion.*

_____ **a.** The iris is the prettiest part of the eye.

_____ **b.** The pupil controls how much light gets into the eye.

_____ **c.** Cones help us see colors in bright light.

3. Making Correct Inferences

Two of the statements below are correct *inferences,* or reasonable guesses, that are based on information in the article. The other statement is an incorrect, or faulty, inference. Label the statements **C** for *correct* inference and **I** for *incorrect* inference.

_____ **a.** Without cones, we would probably see only in black and white.

_____ **b.** The iris relaxes in bright sunlight to let more light in.

_____ **c.** Without the help of the brain, we could not see.

4. Understanding Main Ideas

One of the statements below expresses the main idea of the article. Another statement is too general, or too broad. The other explains only part of the article; it is too narrow. Label the statements **M** for *main idea,* **B** for *too broad,* and **N** for *too narrow.*

_____ **a.** Bright light bleaches the pigment in the rods and makes it stop working.

_____ **b.** Along with the brain, each part of the eye does a job that helps us see.

_____ **c.** Without eyes, we could not see.

5. Responding to the Article

Complete the following sentences in your own words:

One of the things I did best while reading "A Journey Through the Eye" was

_____

_____

I think that I did this well because _____

_____

_____

D. Expanding Vocabulary

Content-Area Words

Read each item carefully. Write on the line the word that best completes each sentence.

1. Organs such as the _____, liver, and eyes do important jobs in the body.

   brain   toenails   hair

2. The muscles in my _____ help me jump and run.

   eyes   face   legs

3. When the cornea focuses the light deep into the eye, it _____ it into a certain spot.

   swings   points   wraps

4. Nerve cells send _____ to the brain.

   notes   signals   letters

5. Pigment makes something appear _____.

   colorful   dangerous   ugly

Academic English

In the article "A Journey Through the Eye," you learned that *images* means "the mind's pictures of things." *Images* can also mean "pictures of people or things," as in the following sentence.

   An artist paints images onto a canvas.

Complete the sentence below.

1. Photographs are *images* taken with a _____

Now use the word *images* in a sentence of your own.

2. _____

You also learned that *adapt* means "to change in order to become used to different conditions." *Adapt* can also mean "to change in order to serve a different purpose," as in the following sentence.

   The editors will adapt the book for younger readers.

Complete the sentence below.

3. I hope that we *adapt* the story to make it into a _____

Now use the word *adapt* in two sentences of your own.

4. _____

5. _____

 Share your new sentences with a partner.

Herbs: Plants of Many Uses

Before You Read

Tip! **Think about what you know.** Read the title and the first two sentences of the article on the opposite page. Can you name an herb that your family uses in cooking?

Vocabulary

The content-area and academic English words below appear in "Herbs: Plants of Many Uses." Read the definitions and the example sentences.

Content-Area Words

fragrances (frā′grəns iz) sweet or pleasing smells
  Example: The flowers in the garden gave off wonderful *fragrances*.

illnesses (il′nis iz) diseases or sicknesses
  Example: Doctors help people with *illnesses* to get better.

rotting (rot′ing) the decaying or spoiling of a once-living thing
  Example: The *rotting* apples were soft and brown.

climate (klī′mit) weather conditions in a certain area over time
  Example: The island has a warm *climate* with very little rainfall.

laboratories (lab′rə tôr′ēz) places where scientific experiments or tests are done
  Example: The scientist performs experiments in his *laboratories*.

Academic English

chemicals (kem′i kəlz) substances that cause and experience changes
  Example: Scientists add *chemicals* to some foods to make them last longer.

aid (ād) to provide help
  Example: My job at the large park is to *aid* people who are lost.

Complete the sentences below that contain the content-area and academic English words above. Use the spaces provided. The first one has been done for you.

1. The *fragrances* of the oranges and lemons made us <u>want to eat them</u>_____.

2. The *rotting* tree had to be _____.

3. The *chemicals* affected the water by _____.

4. We studied the *climate* of Antarctica, including its _____.

5. The organization will *aid* homeless people by _____.

6. *Laboratories* are not good places to play because _____.

7. People with *illnesses* may need medicine to _____.

 Now skim the article and look for other words that are new to you. Write each new word and its definition in the Personal Dictionary.

While You Read

Tip! **Think about why you read.** People use herbs to help treat diseases and illnesses. Do you think it would be useful to know which herbs help to cure certain illnesses? As you read, think about how you might use this information.

Herbs: Plants of Many Uses

1   For thousands of years, people have used plants in many ways. Herbs are plants that were often used to flavor food and to treat, or cure, people who were sick. Herbs have also been used as beauty products, **fragrances,** and dyes, or colors. People also ate herbs for good health. Herbs can come from many kinds of plants, 5 including trees, shrubs, grasses, and flowering plants. Herbs can also come from different plant parts. They can come from roots, stems, leaves, or flowers.

Old Chinese and Egyptian writings tell how people used herbs thousands of years ago. Egyptians used herbs in many ways. Herbs were used in food, on the body, and for religious reasons. In China the emperors, or rulers, Shen Nung and 10 Huang Ti made medicine from herbs. They were two of the first people to use and study Chinese herbal medicine, or medicine made from herbs. Today, people in many parts of the world use Chinese herbal medicine for many kinds of **illnesses.**

People in India have been using herbs as medicine for nearly 5,000 years. Also, in India, many sweet-smelling perfumes and beauty products are made with herbs. 15 And herbs are used in cooking to season, or add flavor to, Indian food.

Hundreds of years ago, European people also had important reasons for putting herbs in their food. They used herbs to help the body break down, or digest, food and to hide the taste of **rotting** meat and fish. Native Americans also have been eating and using herbs for hundreds of years. Some of the ways they use herbs to 20 treat diseases are used now by people all over the world.

In the 19th century, the ways people used herbs as medicines began to change in Europe and in the United States. Scientists began to study the **chemicals** found in plants that **aid** people in staying healthy. Using herbs to treat illnesses can be difficult. Each plant produces a different dose, or amount, of medicine. The 25 season, **climate,** and soil all affect the strength of an herb. If people take too much of an herbal medicine, they can get sick—or even die.

Today scientists and workers make medicines from plants in **laboratories.** Doctors can give exact doses of these medicines. People can be sure that the dose is a safe amount to use. Other useful substances, or products, are also made from 30 herbs. Chamomile shampoo, verbena tea, and aloe vera skin lotion are herbal products. People all over the world use herbal products such as these every day.

CONTENT CONNECTION

The Egyptians used herbs on their bodies. How do people today use herbs on their bodies?

LANGUAGE CONNECTION

Labs is the short form of *laboratories.* An animal doctor is a *veterinarian* or *vet.* What other words have short forms?

After You Read

A. Organizing Ideas

How are herbs used? Complete the web below. In each circle, write down one way herbs are used today or have been used in the past. Refer to the article to help you. One circle has been done for you.

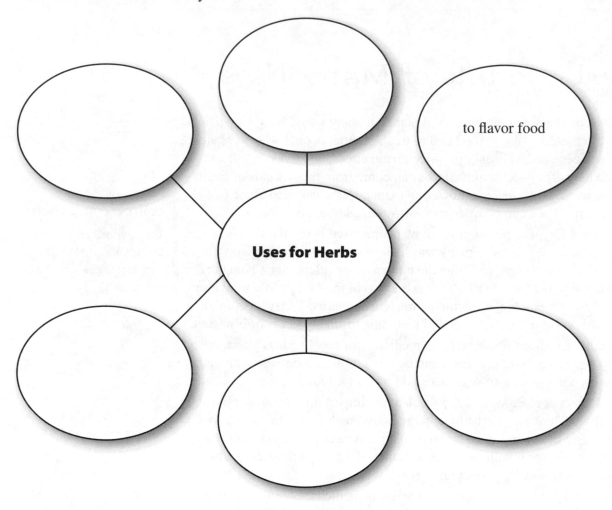

to flavor food

Uses for Herbs

What did you learn about the uses of herbs by completing this web? Write two or more sentences about how herbs have been useful to people. How helpful was this chart as you learned about herbs? Explain your answer.

_____

_____

_____

_____

_____

B. Comprehension Skills

 Think about how to find answers. Look back at different parts of the text. What facts help you figure out how to complete the sentences?

Mark box **a, b,** or **c** with an **X** before the choice that best completes each sentence.

Recalling Facts

1. Herbs have been used to flavor food
   - ☐ **a.** from time to time.
   - ☐ **b.** for thousands of years.
   - ☐ **c.** during the last 200 years.

2. Herbs are often used to
   - ☐ **a.** treat illnesses.
   - ☐ **b.** make food rot.
   - ☐ **c.** fertilize gardens.

3. Herbs come from
   - ☐ **a.** mainly flowers.
   - ☐ **b.** many kinds of plants.
   - ☐ **c.** only leaves and stems.

4. Something new in herbal medicine is
   - ☐ **a.** the use of chamomile to ease pain.
   - ☐ **b.** the scientific study of the chemicals in herbs.
   - ☐ **c.** the use of chemical drugs instead of herbal medicine.

5. Emperors Shen Nung and Huang Ti were two of the first people to study
   - ☐ **a.** herbs in Indian cooking.
   - ☐ **b.** Chinese herbal medicine.
   - ☐ **c.** chemicals found in plants.

Understanding Ideas

1. From the article, you can conclude that the use of herbs as medicine is
   - ☐ **a.** a new idea.
   - ☐ **b.** an idea with a long history.
   - ☐ **c.** an idea that was never popular.

2. People use herbs
   - ☐ **a.** only in China and Egypt.
   - ☐ **b.** in few parts of the world.
   - ☐ **c.** in many parts of the world.

3. Workers in laboratories can make exact doses of herbal medicines because
   - ☐ **a.** they care more about sick people than those of long ago did.
   - ☐ **b.** they are smarter than other people who work with herbal medicines.
   - ☐ **c.** they can take the medicine out of the herbs and measure its strength.

4. From the article, you can conclude that herbs are
   - ☐ **a.** never harmful.
   - ☐ **b.** often flavorful.
   - ☐ **c.** rarely used in cooking.

5. Adding herbs to beauty products is
   - ☐ **a.** a new idea.
   - ☐ **b.** something we do not do anymore.
   - ☐ **c.** something that has been done throughout history.

C. Reading Strategies

1. Recognizing Words in Context

Find the word *exact* in the article. One definition below is closest to the meaning of that word. One definition has the opposite or nearly the opposite meaning. The remaining definition has a meaning that has nothing to do with the other two words. Label the definitions **C** for *closest*, **O** for *opposite* or *nearly opposite*, and **U** for *unrelated*.

_____ **a.** correct or accurate

_____ **b.** confused

_____ **c.** incorrect or indefinite

2. Distinguishing Fact from Opinion

Two of the statements below present *facts,* which can be proved. The other statement is an *opinion*, which expresses someone's thoughts or beliefs. Label the statements **F** for *fact* and **O** for *opinion*.

_____ **a.** Too much of an herbal medicine can harm us.

_____ **b.** People in India have found the best ways to use herbs in cooking.

_____ **c.** The first people to use and study herbal medicine were from China.

3. Making Correct Inferences

Two of the statements below are correct *inferences,* or reasonable guesses, that are based on information in the article. The other statement is an incorrect, or faulty, inference. Label the statements **C** for *correct* inference and **I** for *incorrect* inference.

_____ **a.** Rainfall or hot weather can affect the strength of an herb.

_____ **b.** Herbs are produced only in the leaves of a plant.

_____ **c.** Many of the products we use every day contain herbs.

4. Understanding Main Ideas

One of the statements below expresses the main idea of the article. Another statement is too general, or too broad. The other explains only part of the article; it is too narrow. Label the statements **M** for *main idea*, **B** for *too broad*, and **N** for *too narrow*.

_____ **a.** You may have herbal shampoo in your bathroom.

_____ **b.** People have used plants for thousands of years.

_____ **c.** Herbs have helped people in many ways for thousands of years.

5. Responding to the Article

Complete the following sentences in your own words:
Reading "Herbs: Plants of Many Uses" makes me wonder

_____

I will try to learn more about this by _____

_____

D. Expanding Vocabulary

Content-Area Words

Complete each analogy with a word from the box. Write in the missing word.

illnesses	fragrances	rotting	climate	laboratories

1. sounds : bell :: _____ : perfume

2. fresh : healthy :: _____ : unhealthy

3. toothaches : dentist :: _____ : doctor

4. population : people :: _____ : weather

5. classrooms : teachers :: _____ : scientists

Academic English

In the article "Herbs: Plants of Many Uses," you learned that *chemicals* means "substances that cause and experience changes." *Chemicals* can describe the substances found in plants that can be used to help people stay healthy. *Chemicals* can also describe other substances that cause and experience changes, as in the following sentence.

Liquid cleaners have chemicals that remove dirt and dust.

Complete the sentence below.

1. Gasoline contains *chemicals* that help make it good fuel for_____

Now use the word *chemicals* in a sentence of your own.

2. _____

You also learned that *aid* is a verb that means "to provide help." *Aid* can also be a noun that means "help or assistance," as in the following sentence.

Police and firefighters provide aid for people when there are accidents.

Complete the sentence below.

3. If you need emergency *aid* after an accident, you might call for_____

Now use the word *aid* in two sentences of your own.

4. _____

5. _____

 Share your new sentences with a partner.

Before You Read

 Think about what you know. Read the lesson title above. Think about how you use electricity every day.

Vocabulary

The content-area and academic English words below appear in "Early Discoveries in Electricity." Read the definitions and the example sentences.

Content-Area Words

discovery (dis kuv′ər ē) something new that has not been known or found before
> *Example:* In 1930 people were excited about the *discovery* of the planet Pluto.

amber (am′bər) clear yellow or brown hard material formed from the sap of pine trees
> *Example:* The necklace contained a piece of beautiful yellow *amber*.

matter (mat′ər) anything that takes up space and can be weighed
> *Example:* All things are made up of tiny pieces of *matter*.

continuous (kən tin′ū əs) not stopping
> *Example:* The mother wanted to stop the *continuous* cries of her baby.

current (kur′ənt) streams of air, water, or electricity that flow in a certain direction
> *Example:* We watched as the water *current* moved the leaf down the river.

Academic English

device (di vīs′) a machine or tool created for a certain purpose
> *Example:* The vacuum cleaner is a *device* that we use to clean the carpet.

portion (pôr′shən) one part of a whole
> *Example:* The child ate a small *portion* of the large pizza.

Rate each vocabulary word according to the following scale. Write a number next to each content-area and academic English word.

4   I have never seen the word before.

3   I have seen the word but do not know what it means.

2   I know what the word means when I read it.

1   I use the word myself in speaking or writing.

 Now skim the article and look for other words that are new to you. Write each new word and its definition in the Personal Dictionary.

While You Read

 Think about why you read. Which devices in your home use batteries? Who made the first battery? As you read, try to find the answer.

EARLY DISCOVERIES IN
Electricity

1   Thousands of years ago in Greece, the scientist Thales made an interesting **discovery.** Thales rubbed a piece of **amber** and saw that bird feathers stuck to it. When Thales saw the feathers sticking to the amber, he was seeing static electricity at work. Today we know that static electricity is all around us. For example, think
5 about what happens when you rub a balloon on a shirt or sweater. When you hold the balloon above someone's head, that person's hair stands up straight.

    Static electricity occurs when there is activity, or motion, within the smallest type of **matter.** All things are made up of tiny pieces of matter, or particles, called atoms. Inside atoms there are even smaller particles, called electrons. Electrons
10 have a negative charge. The negative charge makes electrons pull on things that have a positive charge. This pull between positive and negative charges causes amber to pull feathers toward itself, and a balloon to pull hair toward itself.

    Most of the electricity we use today is made of a flow of electrons that does not stop. These nonstop, or **continuous,** moving electrons make up an electric **current.**
15 Some of the most important early discoveries about electric currents were made by Benjamin Franklin, an American. Through his experiments, Franklin showed several important facts about electric currents. One of Franklin's experiments showed that lightning is an example of an electric current that occurs in nature.

    About 200 years ago, the Italian scientist Alessandro Volta created a **device,** or
20 machine, that could produce a continuous flow of electric current. Before then people could make only a quick burst of electricity with a machine called a generator. They had to turn a crank, or handle, with their hands to run the generator. They could store a tiny **portion** of this electric burst in a container called a Leyden jar.

    With Volta's device, it was easy to control the power of the current. Volta put
25 together a stack of small, flat circles, or disks, made of the metals zinc and silver. Between the disks, he laid pieces of cloth or thick paper that he had soaked, or wet, with salt water. The salt water let electrons flow between the two metals. The flow of electrons produced an electric current. Volta's device was an electric battery.

    For many years, people thought that Volta was the first person to make a
30 battery. However, an interesting vase found in Iraq might show that Volta's battery was not the first. The vase is about 2,000 years old. It contains a tube made of the metal copper. A rod made of the metal iron is inside the copper tube. Scientists think that this vase is an early battery. The vase shows that people who lived many years ago may have used electricity.

CONTENT CONNECTION

Static electricity can cause things to stick together or pull on other objects. It can also give you a small electric shock. Have you ever touched something and felt a shock? What did you touch?

LANGUAGE CONNECTION

A *generator* works to *generate,* or produce, power. A *blender* works to *blend,* or mix, foods together. Can you think of other machines with names that explain what they do? Hint: Think of the machines that *wash* clothes and dishes.

After You Read

A. Organizing Ideas

What have you learned about early discoveries in electricity? Complete the chart below. In the first column, list important discoveries that have been made about electricity. In the second column, write down an explanation about each of the discoveries. Some have been done for you.

Important Discoveries	Explanations
Bird feathers stick to amber.	The Greek scientist Thales rubbed amber and saw that feathers stuck to it. What he saw was actually static electricity.
Lightning is an electric current.	

How did this chart help you learn more about important discoveries in electricity? Write two or more sentences about what you have learned from this chart. How do you usually organize new information when you read it? Explain your answer.

_____

_____

_____

_____

B. Comprehension Skills

 Think about how to find answers. Look back at what you read. The information is in the text, but you may have to look in several sentences to find it.

Mark box **a, b,** or **c** with an **X** before the choice that best completes each sentence.

Recalling Facts

1. An old clay vase that held an iron rod and a copper tube may have been used
   ☐ **a.** to prepare food.
   ☐ **b.** to make a battery.
   ☐ **c.** to make medicine.

2. Thousands of years ago, static electricity was seen by
   ☐ **a.** Thales.
   ☐ **b.** Alessandro Volta.
   ☐ **c.** Benjamin Franklin.

3. A small particle with a negative charge is called
   ☐ **a.** zinc.
   ☐ **b.** amber.
   ☐ **c.** an electron.

4. Benjamin Franklin proved that lightning is
   ☐ **a.** not electricity.
   ☐ **b.** an electric current.
   ☐ **c.** a stream of protons.

5. Alessandro Volta put together a stack of zinc and silver disks to make
   ☐ **a.** a generator.
   ☐ **b.** an electric battery.
   ☐ **c.** a lightning experiment.

Understanding Ideas

1. From the article, you can conclude that the ways we use electricity today depend mostly on
   ☐ **a.** lightning.
   ☐ **b.** static electricity.
   ☐ **c.** electric currents.

2. Many years ago, people who lived in the region that now includes Iraq probably
   ☐ **a.** knew nothing about electricity.
   ☐ **b.** knew something about electricity.
   ☐ **c.** knew everything about electricity.

3. Light objects stick to rubbed balloons or amber because of
   ☐ **a.** zinc atoms.
   ☐ **b.** static electricity.
   ☐ **c.** a continuous electric current.

4. From the article, you can conclude that the work of scientists years ago
   ☐ **a.** was not important.
   ☐ **b.** led to modern uses of electricity.
   ☐ **c.** seemed important at the time but was later shown to be useless.

5. A continuous flow of electrons produces
   ☐ **a.** solar power.
   ☐ **b.** static electricity.
   ☐ **c.** an electric current.

C. Reading Strategies

1. Recognizing Words in Context

Find the word *occurs* in the article. One definition below is closest to the meaning of that word. One definition has the opposite or nearly the opposite meaning. The remaining definition has a meaning that has nothing to do with the other two words. Label the definitions **C** for *closest*, **O** for *opposite* or *nearly opposite*, and **U** for *unrelated*.

_____ **a.** stops

_____ **b.** falls

_____ **c.** happens

2. Distinguishing Fact from Opinion

Two of the statements below present *facts*, which can be proved. The other statement is an *opinion*, which expresses someone's thoughts or beliefs. Label the statements **F** for *fact* and **O** for *opinion*.

_____ **a.** Volta made an electric battery.

_____ **b.** Franklin discovered that lightning is a form of electricity.

_____ **c.** The battery was the most important invention of the 1800s.

3. Making Correct Inferences

Two of the statements below are correct *inferences,* or reasonable guesses, that are based on information in the article. The other statement is an incorrect, or faulty, inference. Label the statements **C** for *correct* inference and **I** for *incorrect* inference.

_____ **a.** Without the flow of electrons, we would not have electric currents.

_____ **b.** Volta's battery helped replace the hand-cranked generator.

_____ **c.** No one used electricity until Volta invented the battery.

4. Understanding Main Ideas

One of the statements below expresses the main idea of the article. Another statement is too general, or too broad. The other explains only part of the article; it is too narrow. Label the statements **M** for *main idea*, **B** for *too broad*, and **N** for *too narrow*.

_____ **a.** People have experimented with electricity for thousands of years and made important discoveries about it.

_____ **b.** People have known about electricity for a long time.

_____ **c.** Volta used metal disks to make an electric battery.

5. Responding to the Article

Complete the following sentence in your own words:

One thing in "Early Discoveries in Electricity" that I cannot understand is

_____

_____

_____

D. Expanding Vocabulary

Content-Area Words

Cross out one word or phrase in each row that is not related to the word in dark type.

1. **discovery**	invention	new	station	electricity
2. **amber**	yellow	wet	trees	hard
3. **matter**	burst	solid	weight	gas
4. **continuous**	nonstop	colorful	movement	flow
5. **current**	movement	flow	electricity	handle

Academic English

In the article "Early Discoveries in Electricity," you learned that *device* means "a machine or tool created for a certain purpose." *Device* can also mean "a plan or scheme that helps someone accomplish a goal," as in the following sentence.

He used a clever device to sneak past the guard.

Complete the sentence below.

1. To avoid waking up a sleeping baby, you may use a *device* such as _____

Now use the word *device* in a sentence of your own.

2. _____

_____

You also learned that *portion* means "one part of a whole." *Portion* can describe the part of electricity that people can store. *Portion* can also describe other things that are part of a whole, as in the following sentence.

I ate one portion of the pie, which was cut into eight pieces.

Complete the sentence below.

3. You can pour a *portion* of a quart of milk into a _____

Now use the word *portion* in two sentences of your own.

4. _____

5. _____

 Share your new sentences with a partner.

What Makes a Hurricane?

Before You Read

 Think about what you know. Read the title and the first two sentences of the article on the opposite page. Have you ever seen a hurricane on television or read about one in the newspaper?

Vocabulary

The content-area and academic English words below appear in "What Makes a Hurricane?" Read the definitions and the example sentences.

Content-Area Words

equator (i kwā′tər) an imaginary line that cuts Earth into a top half and a bottom half
   Example: The weather is warm and tropical near the *equator*.

air pressure (ār presh′ər) the force caused by the weight of air
   Example: Weather forecasters measure *air pressure* to see whether it is low or high.

damage (dam′ij) harm or injury that causes something to be broken or useless
   Example: The only *damage* to the car was a broken headlight.

flooding (flud′ing) the rising or overflowing of water over land
   Example: After heavy rain, *flooding* from the river destroyed many houses.

waves (wāvz) moving ridges, such as those on the surface of water
   Example: The ocean *waves* crashed onto the beach.

Academic English

intense (in tens′) very strong
   Example: Mary took medicine when the pain in her leg became *intense*.

duration (doo rā′shən) the amount of time something lasts
   Example: The child sat quietly for the *duration* of the movie.

Read again the example sentences that follow the content-area and academic English word definitions. With a partner, discuss the meanings of the words and sentences. Then make up a sentence of your own for each word. Your teacher may wish to discuss your new sentences in class.

 Now skim the article and look for other words that are new to you. Write each new word and its definition in the Personal Dictionary.

While You Read

 Think about why you read. Hurricanes occur often on our planet. Do you think it would be useful to understand how they form? As you read, think about how people might use this information.

What Makes a Hurricane?

1   A hurricane is a powerful storm with strong winds and **intense** rains. The word *hurricane* comes from a word of the Taino people of the Caribbean. The Taino word means "god of evil." It is related to a word in another language that means "god of wind and storm." People also use the words *cyclones* or *typhoons*
5 when they talk about hurricanes. When a hurricane occurs in Asia, people may call it a cyclone or a typhoon. Meteorologists, or scientists who study the weather, often use the words *tropical cyclones* when they talk about hurricanes.

  Hurricanes form over the ocean in places near the **equator.** In order for these storms to form, the air and water must be in certain conditions. The ocean water
10 must be 27 degrees Celsius (80 degrees Fahrenheit) or warmer. The air must be warm and moist, or filled with tiny droplets of water.

  Air is made up of particles, or small pieces of matter. When the air is warm, the particles are far apart. When the air is cold, the particles are closer together. Warm air forms an area with low **air pressure.** Cold air forms a high-pressure area. Hurricanes
15 can form only in places with low-pressure air. Warm ocean waters heat the low-pressure air. This makes the air travel higher and form tall clouds. As the warmed air rises, high-pressure air quickly comes in from the sides. This creates wind.

  The rotation, or turning, of Earth causes the growing storm to spin. If the storm stays over warm water, it keeps growing. If the winds reach a speed of 61 kilometers
20 (38 miles) per hour, meteorologists call the storm a tropical storm. If the winds reach a speed of 119 kilometers (74 miles) per hour, meteorologists call the storm a hurricane.

  A hurricane is shaped like a thick ring with a hollow, or empty, center. The center is called the eye. Inside the eye, the winds are calm and the sky has no clouds. Sometimes people make a mistake by thinking a hurricane is over when the eye passes
25 over them. The eye is surrounded by strong winds and tall thunderclouds that cause heavy rains. The **duration** of a hurricane can be as short as a few hours or as long as a few weeks. It will not stop or get weaker until it moves over cold water or land.

  Hurricanes cause millions of dollars in **damage.** The powerful winds destroy homes, rip roofs off buildings, break windows, knock down trees, and tear down
30 electrical wires. The storm's heavy rains and huge **waves** that are made by the strong winds cause **flooding.** During strong hurricanes, the sea can rise more than 5 meters (16.5 feet) higher than normal. This high water is called a storm surge. The flooding from a hurricane often kills more people than the winds do.

LANGUAGE CONNECTION

Homographs are words that are spelled the same way but have different meanings. You can write in a *form,* or document. Clouds can *form* shapes in the sky. Can you think of another homograph? Hint: Think of what baseball players use to hit the ball.

CONTENT CONNECTION

In 1992 Hurricane Andrew caused between $15 billion and $30 billion in damage. Why do you think the amount was so high?

After You Read

A. Organizing Ideas

How does a hurricane form? Complete the sequence chart below. In each box, write down one thing that helps a hurricane to form. Refer to the article to help you. The first box has been done for you.

Title: _____

```
┌─────────────────────────────────────────┐
│  The ocean water is 80 degrees Fahrenheit or │
│  warmer, and the air is warm and moist.   │
└─────────────────────────────────────────┘
                    ↓
┌─────────────────────────────────────────┐
│                                           │
└─────────────────────────────────────────┘
                    ↓
┌─────────────────────────────────────────┐
│                                           │
└─────────────────────────────────────────┘
                    ↓
┌─────────────────────────────────────────┐
│                                           │
└─────────────────────────────────────────┘
                    ↓
┌─────────────────────────────────────────┐
│                                           │
└─────────────────────────────────────────┘
```

What did this chart help you understand about how a hurricane forms? Write two or more sentences about the way hurricanes form. What other types of information could be recorded in a chart like this one? Explain your answer.

_____

_____

_____

_____

_____

B. Comprehension Skills

Tip! **Think about how to find answers.** Look back at different parts of the text. What facts help you figure out how to complete the sentences?

Mark box **a, b,** or **c** with an **X** before the choice that best completes each sentence.

Recalling Facts

1. Meteorologists call a hurricane a
   - ☐ **a.** tropical storm.
   - ☐ **b.** tropical cyclone.
   - ☐ **c.** spirit of the wind.

2. A hurricane grows weaker when it moves over
   - ☐ **a.** land.
   - ☐ **b.** warm water.
   - ☐ **c.** tropical oceans.

3. A storm surge occurs when
   - ☐ **a.** heavy rains hit land.
   - ☐ **b.** strong winds knock over trees.
   - ☐ **c.** the water in the ocean suddenly gets higher.

4. A hurricane can form only in an area of
   - ☐ **a.** cold, dry air.
   - ☐ **b.** low-pressure air.
   - ☐ **c.** high-pressure air.

5. A storm with heavy rains and winds of at least 119 kilometers per hour is a
   - ☐ **a.** hurricane.
   - ☐ **b.** thunderstorm.
   - ☐ **c.** tropical storm.

Understanding Ideas

1. A storm that has wind speeds of 80 kilometers per hour would be called a
   - ☐ **a.** hurricane.
   - ☐ **b.** storm surge.
   - ☐ **c.** tropical storm.

2. From the article, you can conclude that a hurricane could form
   - ☐ **a.** above an icy lake.
   - ☐ **b.** over a large desert.
   - ☐ **c.** over an ocean.

3. Most people who are killed during hurricanes probably
   - ☐ **a.** drown.
   - ☐ **b.** are burned.
   - ☐ **c.** are struck by flying objects.

4. From the article, you can conclude that hurricanes are storms that
   - ☐ **a.** can kill.
   - ☐ **b.** are harmless.
   - ☐ **c.** are dangerous only sometimes.

5. You can also conclude that hurricanes form
   - ☐ **a.** only in certain places.
   - ☐ **b.** everywhere in the world.
   - ☐ **c.** over every body of water in the world.

C. Reading Strategies

1. Recognizing Words in Context

Find the word *calm* in the article. One definition below is closest to the meaning of that word. One definition has the opposite or nearly the opposite meaning. The remaining definition has a meaning that has nothing to do with the other two words. Label the definitions **C** for *closest*, **O** for *opposite* or *nearly opposite*, and **U** for *unrelated*.

_____ **a.** loud and wild

_____ **b.** quiet and peaceful

_____ **c.** sad and lonely

2. Distinguishing Fact from Opinion

Two of the statements below present *facts*, which can be proved. The other statement is an *opinion*, which expresses someone's thoughts or beliefs. Label the statements **F** for *fact* and **O** for *opinion*.

_____ **a.** Cold air forms a high-pressure area.

_____ **b.** Hurricanes are scary storms.

_____ **c.** The center of a hurricane is called the eye.

3. Making Correct Inferences

Two of the statements below are correct *inferences*, or reasonable guesses, that are based on information in the article. The other statement is an incorrect, or faulty, inference. Label the statements **C** for *correct* inference and **I** for *incorrect* inference.

_____ **a.** People should find a safe place to stay during a hurricane.

_____ **b.** Once the eye of a hurricane passes, people are no longer in danger.

_____ **c.** Without low-pressure air, hurricanes cannot form.

4. Understanding Main Ideas

One of the statements below expresses the main idea of the article. Another statement is too general, or too broad. The other explains only part of the article; it is too narrow. Label the statements **M** for *main idea*, **B** for *too broad*, and **N** for *too narrow*.

_____ **a.** Hurricanes can last for up to a few weeks.

_____ **b.** Hurricanes are powerful storms that need certain air and water conditions in order to develop.

_____ **c.** Hurricanes are storms that can be dangerous.

5. Responding to the Article

Complete the following sentence in your own words:

Before I read "What Makes a Hurricane?" I thought

_____

but now I know _____

_____

D. Expanding Vocabulary

Content-Area Words

Complete each sentence with a word or phrase from the box. Write the missing word or phrase on the line.

| equator | air pressure | flooding | waves | damage |

1. Many of the homes in our town had great _____ from the hurricane.

2. The ocean's huge waves caused _____ in many Florida neighborhoods.

3. In areas of high _____, a hurricane cannot form.

4. Places near the _____ are usually warm all year.

5. The strong winds of the hurricane caused huge _____ to crash onto the beach.

Academic English

In the article "What Makes a Hurricane?" you learned that *intense* means "very strong." *Intense* can describe the strong rains of a hurricane. *Intense* can also describe feelings or emotions that are very strong, as in the following sentence.

   The father felt intense love for his children.

Complete the sentence below.

1. Her dislike of sour candy became *intense* after _____

Now use the word *intense* in a sentence of your own.

2. _____

   _____

You also learned that *duration* means "the amount of time something lasts." *Duration* can describe the amount of time a hurricane lasts. *Duration* can also describe the amount of time other things last, as in the following sentence.

   The duration of one year is twelve months.

Complete the sentence below.

3. The student was able to pay attention for the *duration* of the _____

Now use the word *duration* in two sentences of your own.

4. _____

5. _____

 Share your new sentences with a partner.

Writing a Postcard

Read the postcard. Then complete the sentences. Use words from the Word Bank.

Dear Juanita,

   Hello from space camp! I am having a great time learning what astronauts do. I have floated in a room without _____. The campers have toured the _____ where scientists create and test new _____ that will be used in space. Today we will see a small _____ of a spaceship that has _____ from a meteoroid. I hope you are enjoying this summer as much as I am.

                                    See you soon!

                                    Ana

Word Bank

portion
damage
laboratories
gravity
devices

Juanita Perez
555 Elm Road
Your Town
Your State 55533

Reading an Interview

Read the interview. Circle the word that completes each sentence.

EXCLUSIVE INTERVIEW

Channel 5 Reporter: Could you please explain your discovery to our viewers, Dr. Lim?

Dr. Lim: Certainly. I have discovered an amazing medicine that will (**adapt, aid**) people with many different illnesses.

Channel 5 Reporter: What does the medicine do?

Dr. Lim: It prevents important parts of the body from being damaged when a person is sick. If a person's (**pigments, muscles**) are damaged, it is hard for the person to move. If a person's (**chemicals, nerves**) are damaged, it is hard for the person to feel pain, heat, or cold. This medicine protects these parts and others.

Channel 5 Reporter: What is the medicine made from?

Dr. Lim: The medicine (**comprises, focuses**) many different herbs. They are combined to make the medicine.

Channel 5 Reporter: Does the sick person need to take the medicine every day for the (**fusion, duration**) of the illness?

Dr. Lim: Yes. The medicine works best when the person takes it each night.

Channel 5 Reporter: What a great discovery! Congratulations, Dr. Lim.

Making Connections

Work with a partner. Talk about what the words mean. Write words that go together in the columns below. Then write a name for each group of words.

| intense | flooding | waves | glowing | equator |
| survive | current | climate | images | fragrances |

Group 1	Group 2	Group 3
_____	_____	_____
_____	_____	_____
_____	_____	_____
_____	_____	_____

Use all of the words above in complete sentences of your own. You may wish to use more than one word from each column in one sentence. To help you start writing, think about the groups of words you created. After you write your sentences, read them over. If you find a mistake, correct it.

_____

_____

_____

_____

_____

_____

_____

_____

_____

_____

_____

Before You Read

 Think about what you know. Read the lesson title above. What do you predict the article will be about? What do you think grasslands are?

Vocabulary

The content-area and academic English words below appear in "Where Have All the Grasslands Gone?" Read the definitions and the example sentences.

Content-Area Words

ecosystem (ē′kō sis′təm) plants and animals that live together in an area of nature
 Example: Trees, birds, and bears are all part of the forest's *ecosystem*.

destroyed (di stroid′) ruined or killed
 Example: The forest fire *destroyed* many trees and plants.

fertile (furt′əl) able to produce crops or plants easily and plentifully
 Example: The corn grew well in the *fertile* soil.

government (guv′ərn mənt) people that control a place, such as a city, state, or country
 Example: The *government* of our city uses tax money to keep the streets clean.

erosion (i rō′zhən) the slow wearing away of soil and rock, caused by water or wind
 Example: *Erosion* from the flowing water had smoothed the rocks in the river.

Academic English

restore (ri stôr′) to put something back the way it was before
 Example: She worked hard to *restore* the garden after her dog dug up the flowers.

regions (rē′jənz) parts or areas of something
 Example: Some *regions* of our country have mountains, and others are flat.

Complete the sentences below that contain the content-area and academic English words above. Use the spaces provided. The first one has been done for you.

1. Sharks and other fish are part of the *ecosystem* of _an ocean_____.

2. Desert *regions* do not have much _____.

3. She plans to *restore* the color of the old rocking chair by _____.

4. The strong winds *destroyed* the little cabin by_____.

5. We knew the garden soil was *fertile* because_____.

6. *Erosion* affected the stone statue by_____.

7. Our city *government* makes laws to _____.

 Now skim the article and look for other words that are new to you. Write each new word and its definition in the Personal Dictionary.

While You Read

 Think about why you read. Have you ever seen grasslands? As you read, look for the paragraph that gives another name for grasslands. Look for the reasons that grasslands have changed.

Where Have All the GRASSLANDS Gone?

1   Grasslands in the United States once stretched from the Mississippi River to the Rocky Mountains. The grasslands, also called prairies, were a home for grasses, herbs, birds, rodents, and grazers, or animals that eat grasses. By eating grass, grazers such as buffalo, deer, and elk kept the grasses from getting too long
5   or wild. Fires also helped to maintain grasslands, or keep them healthy. Fires cleared out old or dead grass so that new grass could grow. The plants and animals that lived in the grasslands needed one another to stay alive. For thousands of years, Native Americans were a part of this **ecosystem.** They could find all of the things they needed to live on the grasslands.

10   Today only small areas of grassland are left. Most of the grasslands have been used for farming, covered with roads and cities, or used to raise cattle, such as cows and bulls. What **destroyed** the grasslands that once covered almost half of the country?

     First, pioneers, or the first people other than native groups to explore or live in an area, moved west and found the grasslands. Pioneers thought the **fertile** soil of
15   the grasslands was perfect for farming. They began to farm using machines called plows. A new type of plow helped pioneer farmers cut easily through the thick roots of the grass.

     Buffalo were a second reason for the changes to the grasslands. Buffalo are large, hairy, cowlike mammals with short horns and heavy, strong bodies. Pioneers
20   hunted buffalo for sport. Over 100 years, the number of buffalo went down from about 60 million to 1,000. Without buffalo grazing on the grasslands, certain kinds of plants grew strong and thick. These plants began to crowd out other plants.

     The crops planted in the area were a third reason that the land changed. Without the thick roots of grasses growing in it, the soil had nothing to hold it down during
25   windy winters. In the 1920s, much less rain fell than usual. The dry soil began to blow away in the wind. The U.S. **government** wanted to help stop this soil **erosion.** It began to buy back land from farmers. In 1960 about 1.6 million hectares (4 million acres) of this land became grasslands owned by the government.

     Today people are working to **restore** grasslands. They are trying to help return
30   them to the way they once were. These people carefully plant grasses and other plants that once grew on the prairies. They set controlled fires to learn more about how fires encourage new growth. They bring in buffalo to live and graze on the sites. By studying the grasslands, the people hope to learn as much as they can. They hope to protect the small **regions** of grassland we have left, and to keep them healthy.

LANGUAGE CONNECTION

Graze is a verb that means "to eat grasses." A grazer is an animal that eats grasses. The suffix *-er* changes the verb to a noun. Can you think of other words that use the suffix *-er*? Hint: What do you call someone who runs?

CONTENT CONNECTION

Pioneers hunted buffalo. This is a *cause.* The number of buffalo went down. This is the *effect.* Can you find other places in the article that show cause and effect?

After You Read

A. Organizing Ideas

What has changed the grasslands? Complete the chart below. Write down the causes and effects involved in the destruction of the grasslands. You may have more than one effect for a cause. Refer to the article for help.

Cause	Effect
Pioneers used plows to remove grasses from the soil.	Pioneers used the fertile land for farming, and began to destroy the grasslands.
Pioneer farmers planted crops in the fertile soil where grasses had once grown.	

What does this chart show you about the history of the grasslands? Write two or more sentences about something that changed the grasslands. Tell how you could record information from this article in another way. Explain your answer.

_____

_____

_____

_____

_____

_____

B. Comprehension Skills

 Think about how to find answers. Think about what each sentence means. Try to say it to yourself in your own words before you complete it.

Mark box **a, b,** or **c** with an **X** before the choice that best completes each sentence.

Recalling Facts

1. Grassland once covered
   - ☐ **a.** the world.
   - ☐ **b.** the entire United States.
   - ☐ **c.** almost half of the United States.

2. For thousands of years, the grasslands provided food for
   - ☐ **a.** cattle ranchers.
   - ☐ **b.** pioneer farmers.
   - ☐ **c.** Native Americans.

3. In the 1920s, soil erosion occurred in places where
   - ☐ **a.** buffalo had eaten all the grass.
   - ☐ **b.** grassland had been replaced by crops.
   - ☐ **c.** tall grasses had crowded out other plants.

4. Pioneers moving west
   - ☐ **a.** protected buffalo from hunters.
   - ☐ **b.** found the grasslands to be perfect farmland.
   - ☐ **c.** found that the grasslands were not worth farming.

5. Grassland is made up of
   - ☐ **a.** grasses and herbs.
   - ☐ **b.** swamps and marshes.
   - ☐ **c.** large trees and mountains.

Understanding Ideas

1. If you were walking through a prairie, you would be most likely to see
   - ☐ **a.** a lion.
   - ☐ **b.** a goat.
   - ☐ **c.** a rabbit.

2. According to the article, people can help restore the grasslands by
   - ☐ **a.** hunting buffalo.
   - ☐ **b.** keeping buffalo off protected sites.
   - ☐ **c.** bringing buffalo to live on protected sites.

3. A natural part of a healthy grassland is
   - ☐ **a.** fire.
   - ☐ **b.** plowing.
   - ☐ **c.** ranching.

4. From the article, you can conclude that not all grassland will be restored, because
   - ☐ **a.** buffalo have become extinct.
   - ☐ **b.** some people want to use the land for other things.
   - ☐ **c.** most of the soil has been poisoned with weed killers.

5. From the article, you can conclude that
   - ☐ **a.** all grassland will disappear forever.
   - ☐ **b.** the grasslands will never again be in danger.
   - ☐ **c.** some grassland will be restored and protected.

C. Reading Strategies

1. Recognizing Words in Context

Find the word *studying* in the article. One definition below is closest to the meaning of that word. One definition has the opposite or nearly the opposite meaning. The remaining definition has a meaning that has nothing to do with the other two words. Label the definitions **C** for *closest*, **O** for *opposite* or *nearly opposite*, and **U** for *unrelated*.

_____ **a.** looking closely at

_____ **b.** ignoring

_____ **c.** feeding

2. Distinguishing Fact from Opinion

Two of the statements below present *facts,* which can be proved. The other statement is an *opinion,* which expresses someone's thoughts or beliefs. Label the statements **F** for *fact* and **O** for *opinion.*

_____ **a.** The grasslands are more beautiful now than they were 100 years ago.

_____ **b.** Farming is one reason the grasslands almost disappeared.

_____ **c.** Fires help, rather than destroy, grasslands.

3. Making Correct Inferences

Two of the statements below are correct *inferences,* or reasonable guesses, that are based on information in the article. The other statement is an incorrect, or faulty, inference. Label the statements **C** for *correct* inference and **I** for *incorrect* inference.

_____ **a.** The grasslands need grazers, such as buffalo, to stay healthy.

_____ **b.** Farming was good for pioneers but bad for the grasslands.

_____ **c.** The government has given up on the grasslands and left them alone.

4. Understanding Main Ideas

One of the statements below expresses the main idea of the article. Another statement is too general, or too broad. The other explains only part of the article; it is too narrow. Label the statements **M** for *main idea,* **B** for *too broad,* and **N** for *too narrow.*

_____ **a.** Most of the American grasslands have disappeared.

_____ **b.** The use of plows is one reason the grasslands were almost destroyed.

_____ **c.** Huge areas of American grassland were destroyed by farmers and hunters, but today people are working to restore and protect them.

5. Responding to the Article

Complete the following sentence in your own words:

From reading "Where Have All the Grasslands Gone?" I have learned

_____

_____

D. Expanding Vocabulary

Content-Area Words

Read each item carefully. Write on the line the word or phrase that best completes each sentence.

1. For thousands of years, the ecosystem of the _____ included plants, animals, and Native American people.

   jungle   grasslands   swamp

2. The plow destroyed the roots of grasses by _____ them.

   cutting   eating   burning

3. Soil that is fertile is perfect for _____.

   plowing   digging   farming

4. The thick _____ of prairie grasses help prevent soil erosion.

   leaves   roots   stems

5. The U.S. government wants to _____ restore the grasslands.

   cry   plant crops   help

Academic English

In the article "Where Have All the Grasslands Gone?" you learned that *restore* means "to put something back the way it was before." *Restore* can also mean "to return something that has been taken," as in the following sentence.

The police had to restore the stolen car to its owner.

Complete the sentence below.

1. Because the bank robber felt guilty, he decided to *restore* the money to_____

Now use the word *restore* in a sentence of your own.

2. _____

You also learned that *regions* means "parts or areas of something." *Regions* can describe parts of a country, such as grasslands. *Regions* can also describe parts of the body, as in the following sentence.

The chest is one of the upper regions of the body.

Complete the sentence below.

3. The ankle and the foot are in the lower *regions* of_____

Now use the word *regions* in two sentences of your own.

4. _____

5. _____

 Share your new sentences with a partner.

Before You Read

 Think about what you know. Skim the article on the opposite page. Do you think scorpions are arachnids?

Vocabulary

The content-area and academic English words below appear in "Arachnids." Read the definitions and the example sentences.

Content-Area Words

joints (joints) places where two bones meet or join, such as a knee or an elbow
Example: My knee *joints* were very sore and swollen after I fell.

abdomen (ab'də mən) the main part of the body that contains organs in the middle region
Example: The stomach is an organ in the *abdomen*.

protein (prō'tēn) a material in all living cells that people need for health
Example: The cheese in my sandwich contains the *protein* my body needs.

pincers (pin'sərz) claws used for grabbing and holding
Example: The lobster pinched my fingers with its *pincers*.

prey (prā) an animal that is hunted or killed for food
Example: Frogs look for flies to eat, because flies are *prey* for frogs.

Academic English

features (fē'chərz) parts of the body that people see or notice
Example: The robber's blue eyes and long nose were two *features* that showed through his mask.

encounter (en koun'tər) to meet or come across something
Example: Sometimes I *encounter* my neighbor when I go for a walk.

Do any of the words above seem related? Sort the seven vocabulary words into two or more categories. Write the words down on note cards or in a chart. Words may fit into more than one group. You may wish to work with a partner for this activity.

Dictionary Now skim the article and look for other words that are new to you. Write each new word and its definition in the Personal Dictionary.

While You Read

Tip! **Think about why you read.** Do you like spiders? Many people do not like them. As you read, think about why that might be.

Arachnids

1 An arachnid is an animal that has **joints** in its legs, a tough skeleton on the outside of its body, and no backbone, or spine. Insects, such as flies and ants, also have these body **features.** However, arachnids have several other similarities. They have eight legs, simple eyes, and a body made up of one or two sections.

5 They eat liquid food. They often live alone on land and kill their food. Spiders, scorpions, ticks, mites, and daddy longlegs are all arachnids.

Like most other arachnids, spiders have eight walking legs, hollow teeth called fangs, and palps. Palps are fingerlike parts that an arachnid uses for touching and tasting. The two sections of a spider's body are called the head and the **abdomen.**

10 All spiders spin a silky material made from **protein,** but not all spiders use the material to make webs. Some spiders, such as wolf spiders, hunt insects. Other spiders wait for insects to land in their webs. Spiders kill insects in two ways. Some spiders wrap the insects in silk and tear them apart. Other spiders kill insects with liquid poison called venom. The venom comes out of their hollow

15 fangs. It melts the insides of the insect, and then the spider sucks out the liquid.

You will know when you **encounter** a scorpion because it has front **pincers,** like a lobster's, and a curved tail. The tail has a poisonous stinger on the end. The sting can be very painful to humans. A stinger is a sharp organ that scorpions use to squirt poison into their **prey.** A scorpion uses its stinger mostly to protect,

20 or defend, itself when it is in danger. Scorpions come out at night and wait for prey to come close. They eat anything they can catch—mostly insects and other arachnids. Scorpions sometimes use their stingers to kill larger prey. When they catch smaller prey, they just hold it tightly and eat it. Scorpions tear their prey into pieces and cover the pieces with liquid called digestive juices. These juices break

25 down food into liquid that the body can use. Then the scorpions suck the liquid into their stomachs.

Ticks and mites are arachnids that have only one body section. Most ticks and mites have six legs when they hatch, or come out of their eggs. They grow another pair of legs as they turn into adults. Ticks and mites often feed on other living

30 things. They have mouth parts for sucking blood and juices from animals that are alive. Ticks eat the blood of reptiles, birds, and mammals. Mites eat blood, skin, and other materials from animals and plants.

Daddy longlegs, also called harvestmen, are special arachnids. Most arachnids can eat only liquid foods, but daddy longlegs can also eat small pieces of solid food. Also,

35 daddy longlegs run after their insect prey instead of trapping it or waiting for it. Daddy longlegs are also different from most arachnids in that they can eat plants.

LANGUAGE CONNECTION

Some animals have names that give clues to how they look. The name *daddy longlegs* tells people that this arachnid has long legs. What do you think a red-winged blackbird looks like?

CONTENT CONNECTION

Ticks are arachnids that attach themselves to larger animals and suck their blood. Ticks can also carry diseases. Do you think that ticks are dangerous to people?

After You Read

A. Organizing Ideas

What are the different types of arachnids? Complete the chart below. In each box, write the name of a type of arachnid on the line. Below the line, list facts about that arachnid. Use the information in the article to help you. Some items have been done for you.

Arachnids

_____

- have eight legs, fangs, and palps.

- have bodies with two sections: the head and the abdomen.
- spin silk and sometimes use it to make webs.
- sometimes use venom to poison their prey.

Scorpions _____

- _____

- _____

- _____

- _____

Ticks and mites _____

- _____

- _____

- _____

- _____

_____

- _____

- _____

- _____

- _____

How did the chart help you compare different types of arachnids? Write two or more sentences about how different types of arachnids are alike and different. What other type of chart could help you compare the types of arachnids? Explain your answer.

_____

_____

_____

B. Comprehension Skills

Tip! **Think about how to find answers.** Read each sentence below. Underline the words that will help you figure out how to complete each item.

Mark box **a, b,** or **c** with an **X** before the choice that best completes each sentence.

Recalling Facts

1. An animal that has eight walking legs and eats liquid food is
   - ☐ **a.** a squid.
   - ☐ **b.** an insect.
   - ☐ **c.** an arachnid.

2. Arachnids have
   - ☐ **a.** no eyes.
   - ☐ **b.** simple eyes.
   - ☐ **c.** compound eyes.

3. All spiders
   - ☐ **a.** eat plants.
   - ☐ **b.** make webs.
   - ☐ **c.** spin a silky material.

4. An arachnid that eats plants is a
   - ☐ **a.** spider.
   - ☐ **b.** scorpion.
   - ☐ **c.** daddy longlegs.

5. A scorpion
   - ☐ **a.** builds a web to catch prey.
   - ☐ **b.** waits for its prey to come near.
   - ☐ **c.** always uses its stinger to kill prey.

Understanding Ideas

1. From the article, you can conclude that all insects and spiders have
   - ☐ **a.** four legs.
   - ☐ **b.** three body parts.
   - ☐ **c.** tough skeletons on the outside of their bodies.

2. The use of poison to kill prey is most common in
   - ☐ **a.** all arachnids.
   - ☐ **b.** animals with fur.
   - ☐ **c.** spiders and scorpions.

3. From the article, you can conclude that the word *tear* means
   - ☐ **a.** "spin."
   - ☐ **b.** "chew."
   - ☐ **c.** "rip apart."

4. You can also conclude that almost all adult arachnids
   - ☐ **a.** have eight legs.
   - ☐ **b.** are dangerous to humans.
   - ☐ **c.** kill their prey with venom.

5. By grouping animals according to the ways they look, we can often understand
   - ☐ **a.** how animals find food.
   - ☐ **b.** how some animals are alike and how they are different.
   - ☐ **c.** how humans are different from other animals.

C. Reading Strategies

1. Recognizing Words in Context

Find the word *feed* in the article. One definition below is closest to the meaning of that word. One definition has the opposite or nearly the opposite meaning. The remaining definition has a meaning that has nothing to do with the other two words. Label the definitions **C** for *closest*, **O** for *opposite* or *nearly opposite*, and **U** for *unrelated*.

_____ **a.** find

_____ **b.** starve

_____ **c.** eat

2. Distinguishing Fact from Opinion

Two of the statements below present *facts*, which can be proved. The other statement is an *opinion*, which expresses someone's thoughts or beliefs. Label the statements **F** for *fact* and **O** for *opinion*.

_____ **a.** Ticks and mites are arachnids that have only one body section.

_____ **b.** All spiders spin silk, but not all spiders make webs.

_____ **c.** Spiders are very smart hunters.

3. Making Correct Inferences

Two of the statements below are correct *inferences,* or reasonable guesses, that are based on information in the article. The other statement is an incorrect, or faulty, inference. Label the statements **C** for *correct* inference and **I** for *incorrect* inference.

_____ **a.** The bodies of most ticks and mites change as they turn into adults.

_____ **b.** Large animals are not bothered by scorpion stings.

_____ **c.** Scorpions and lobsters have some similar body parts.

4. Understanding Main Ideas

One of the statements below expresses the main idea of the article. Another statement is too general, or too broad. The other explains only part of the article; it is too narrow. Label the statements **M** for *main idea*, **B** for *too broad*, and **N** for *too narrow*.

_____ **a.** Arachnids are alike in many ways, but each type of arachnid also has special features that make it different from the others.

_____ **b.** Scorpions use their stingers to protect themselves.

_____ **c.** Arachnids have many of the same features.

5. Responding to the Article

Complete the following sentence in your own words:
Reading "Arachnids" made me feel

_____

_____

D. Expanding Vocabulary

Content-Area Words

Complete each sentence with a word from the box. Write the missing word on the line.

joints	abdomen	protein	pincers	prey

1. The _____ in my legs hurt after I ran the race.

2. A swimming fish is _____ for a hungry wild bear.

3. When you look at a spider's web, you see tiny strings made of _____.

4. The lobster used its _____ to pull apart its food.

5. The _____ of an insect contains many of its organs.

Academic English

In the article "Arachnids," you learned that *features* is a noun that means "parts of the body that people see or notice." *Features* can also be a verb that means "shows something so that people see or notice it," as in the following sentence.

The movie features one of my favorite actors.

Complete the sentence below.

1. The school talent show *features* students who can _____

Now use the word *features* in a sentence of your own.

2. _____

_____

You also learned that *encounter* is a verb that means "to meet or come across something." *Encounter* can also be a noun that means "a meeting," as in the following sentence.

I was frightened after my encounter with a snake in the forest.

Complete the sentence below.

3. An *encounter* between students and teachers usually happens at _____

Now use the word *encounter* in two sentences of your own.

4. _____

5. _____

 Share your new sentences with a partner.

Before You Read

 Think about what you know. Read the title and the first three sentences of the article on the opposite page. Think about what you already know about astronauts.

Vocabulary

The content-area and academic English words below appear in "Training to Be an Astronaut." Read the definitions and the example sentences.

Content-Area Words

recruits (ri krōōts′) new members of a group or team
  Example: The new *recruits* had to learn how to do their jobs.

mission control (mish′ən kən trōl′) the people on Earth who talk with and help astronauts in space
  Example: The astronaut called *mission control* for help with the problem.

control panels (kən trōl′ pan′əlz) areas with buttons and dials that control a machine
  Example: Control panels on airplanes have many buttons that do different jobs.

weightlessness (wāt′lis nis) the feeling of having little or no weight
  Example: Astronauts in space feel *weightlessness* when they float in the air.

mission (mish′ən) a specific job that a person or group must do
  Example: The detective's *mission* is to find the lost computer.

Academic English

undergo (un′dər gō′) to go through or experience something
  Example: I must *undergo* a health exam before I can play on the soccer team.

simulate (sim′yə lāt′) to feel or look like something else
  Example: This video game can *simulate* a real car race.

Rate each vocabulary word according to the following scale. Write a number next to each content-area and academic English word.

4 I have never seen the word before.

3 I have seen the word but do not know what it means.

2 I know what the word means when I read it.

1 I use the word myself in speaking or writing.

 Now skim the article and look for other words that are new to you. Write each new word and its definition in the Personal Dictionary.

While You Read

 Think about why you read. Do you think you could be an astronaut? As you read, think about the work astronauts do to prepare for a trip into space.

The Learning Café
Lethbridge College

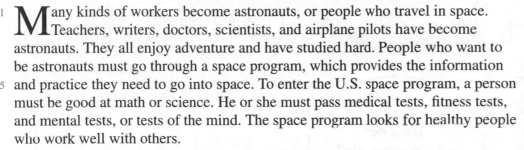
TRAINING TO BE
an Astronaut

1 Many kinds of workers become astronauts, or people who travel in space. Teachers, writers, doctors, scientists, and airplane pilots have become astronauts. They all enjoy adventure and have studied hard. People who want to be astronauts must go through a space program, which provides the information and practice they need to go into space. To enter the U.S. space program, a person
5 must be good at math or science. He or she must pass medical tests, fitness tests, and mental tests, or tests of the mind. The space program looks for healthy people who work well with others.

The National Aeronautics and Space Administration, or NASA, runs the space
10 program. A person invited to join the space program does not become an astronaut right away. New **recruits** train in classrooms for a year. They learn how a space shuttle (a spacecraft that can hold people) works. They study weather, space, and computers. If they do well, they can become astronauts.

A new astronaut must **undergo** years of special training. New astronauts might
15 work with scientists who make shuttle machines and equipment. They might also work with **mission control** to talk to crews in space. A crew is a group of people who operate a spacecraft. This kind of work helps new astronauts learn and practice useful skills. They will use these skills when they go into space.

Some astronauts know how to fly fast airplanes called jets when they enter the
20 space program. Pilots, or people who fly planes, stay good at flying by practicing often. Astronauts who do not know how to fly planes must learn to be pilots. All astronauts need to learn how to fly a space shuttle by using the shuttle **control panels.** They practice landing an aircraft similar to the space shuttle to learn how to bring it safely down to the ground.

25 Astronauts work underwater to **simulate** moving around in a space suit. A space suit is special clothing that astronauts wear to keep their bodies safe in space. To feel **weightlessness,** astronauts ride in a special jet. The jet climbs high into the air and then dives about 3 kilometers (2 miles). During these long dives, astronauts feel weightless for 30 to 60 seconds. The jet might dive 40 times in a
30 day. Some astronauts feel sick to their stomachs after doing this for a while.

Astronauts have to be ready for any kind of emergency, or surprise problem, on a **mission.** They learn many survival skills, or ways to keep themselves alive in difficult situations. Only after they train, work, and practice with crew members for years can astronauts go on a mission and do important experiments in space.

CONTENT CONNECTION

Astronauts learn skills such as how to fly planes, operate special equipment, and move in a space suit. What skills does a firefighter need? An athlete? A zookeeper?

LANGUAGE CONNECTION

Antonyms are words that have opposite meanings. The words *easy* and *difficult* are antonyms. *Safe* and *dangerous* are also antonyms. Can you think of antonyms for *love, healthy,* and *new?*

After You Read

A. Organizing Ideas

How do astronauts train? Complete the web below. In each oval, write down one way astronauts train before they go into space. Use the information in the article to help you. The first oval has been done for you.

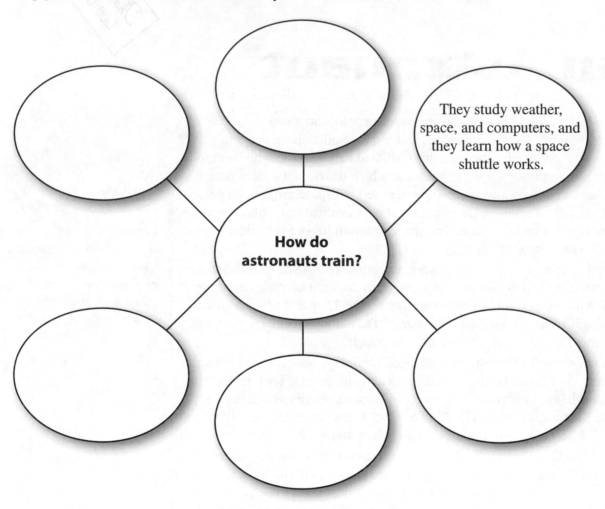

How did this web help you learn about the ways astronauts train? Write two or more sentences about how astronauts train. Did this web help you organize your information clearly? Explain your answer.

_____

_____

_____

_____

B. Comprehension Skills

 Think about how to find answers. Look back at what you read. The information is in the text, but you may have to look in several sentences to find it.

Mark box **a, b,** or **c** with an **X** before the choice that best completes each sentence.

Recalling Facts

1. To join the space program, a person must
   - ☐ **a.** be a teacher.
   - ☐ **b.** pass medical and fitness tests.
   - ☐ **c.** already have been an astronaut.

2. New recruits spend their first year in the space program in
   - ☐ **a.** space.
   - ☐ **b.** classrooms.
   - ☐ **c.** a weightless room.

3. Learning to fly and land a shuttle is a skill
   - ☐ **a.** only shuttle pilots learn.
   - ☐ **b.** all of the astronauts learn.
   - ☐ **c.** none of the astronauts learn.

4. Astronauts can go on a shuttle mission
   - ☐ **a.** as soon as they join the space program.
   - ☐ **b.** after they have been in the space program for two months.
   - ☐ **c.** after they have been in the space program for years.

5. Astronauts work underwater to
   - ☐ **a.** get ready for liftoffs.
   - ☐ **b.** practice holding their breath.
   - ☐ **c.** learn how to move in a space suit.

Understanding Ideas

1. One skill an astronaut learns in the space program is how to
   - ☐ **a.** ride a bicycle.
   - ☐ **b.** speak different languages.
   - ☐ **c.** fly a shuttle by using the shuttle control panels.

2. Astronauts fly on special jets to
   - ☐ **a.** feel weightlessness.
   - ☐ **b.** relax and have fun.
   - ☐ **c.** get ready for their physical exams.

3. From the article, you can conclude that unhealthy people
   - ☐ **a.** can be good astronauts.
   - ☐ **b.** often become astronauts.
   - ☐ **c.** will not be chosen to become astronauts.

4. A new astronaut in the space program
   - ☐ **a.** works in the space program to gain knowledge.
   - ☐ **b.** flies on a shuttle mission right away for practice.
   - ☐ **c.** does not need to learn new things.

5. From the article, you can conclude that astronauts have
   - ☐ **a.** no training.
   - ☐ **b.** little training.
   - ☐ **c.** a lot of training.

C. Reading Strategies

1. Recognizing Words in Context

Find the word *adventure* in the article. One definition below is closest to the meaning of that word. One definition has the opposite or nearly the opposite meaning. The remaining definition has a meaning that has nothing to do with the other two words. Label the definitions **C** for *closest*, **O** for *opposite* or *nearly opposite*, and **U** for *unrelated*.

_____ **a.** routine event

_____ **b.** creative activity

_____ **c.** risky action

2. Distinguishing Fact from Opinion

Two of the statements below present *facts,* which can be proved. The other statement is an *opinion*, which expresses someone's thoughts or beliefs. Label the statements **F** for *fact* and **O** for *opinion*.

_____ **a.** Only healthy people who get along with others can become astronauts.

_____ **b.** Writers make the best astronauts.

_____ **c.** You do not have to be a pilot to become an astronaut.

3. Making Correct Inferences

Two of the statements below are correct *inferences,* or reasonable guesses, that are based on information in the article. The other statement is an incorrect, or faulty, inference. Label the statements **C** for *correct* inference and **I** for *incorrect* inference.

_____ **a.** Astronauts know how to stay alive in dangerous situations.

_____ **b.** A healthy doctor could possibly become an astronaut.

_____ **c.** The job of mission control is to fly a space shuttle.

4. Understanding Main Ideas

One of the statements below expresses the main idea of the article. Another statement is too general, or too broad. The other explains only part of the article; it is too narrow. Label the statements **M** for *main idea*, **B** for *too broad*, and **N** for *too narrow*.

_____ **a.** Astronauts train underwater to feel like they are in space.

_____ **b.** After years of many difficult tests and training programs, astronauts are ready for a space mission.

_____ **c.** Astronauts must train for a long time.

5. Responding to the Article

Complete the following sentence in your own words:

Reading "Training to Be an Astronaut" reminded me of

_____

_____

D. Expanding Vocabulary

Content-Area Words

Cross out one word or phrase in each row that is not related to the word in dark type.

1. recruits	parachute	new	team	people
2. mission control	Earth	talk	astronauts	doctors
3. control panels	shuttle	buttons	easy	machine
4. weightlessness	float	gravity	light	work
5. mission	job	space	stretch	astronaut

Academic English

In the article "Training to Be an Astronaut," you learned that *undergo* means "to go through or experience something." *Undergo* can describe experiences that people must go through. *Undergo* can also describe experiences that nonliving things go through, as in the following sentence.

The hospital will undergo construction that will add more rooms to the first floor.

Complete the sentence below.

1. The chemicals in my experiment will *undergo* a change when I_____

Now use the word *undergo* in a sentence of your own.

2. _____

_____

You also learned that *simulate* means "to feel or look like something else." *Simulate* can refer to how working underwater feels like working in space. *Simulate* can also refer to other things that look or feel like something else, as in the following sentence.

Globes and maps simulate the surface of Earth.

Complete the sentence below.

3. Some lizards can *simulate* _____

Now use the word *simulate* in two sentences of your own.

4. _____

5. _____

 Share your new sentences with a partner.

Why Is Sleep Good for Us?

Before You Read

 Think about what you know. Read the first paragraph of the article on the opposite page. Have you ever had a night with very little sleep? How did you feel the next day?

Vocabulary

The content-area and academic English words below appear in "Why Is Sleep Good for Us?" Read the definitions and the example sentences.

Content-Area Words

moody (mōō′dē) having emotions, or feelings, that change often
> *Example:* The *moody* child was happy one minute and grumpy the next.

recover (ri kuv′ər) to get back to a normal state
> *Example:* You must rest while you *recover* from your illness.

stages (stāj′iz) lengths of time or steps in a process
> *Example:* One of the *stages* of building a house is cutting the wood.

dreaming (drēm′ing) thinking, feeling, or seeing pictures while asleep
> *Example:* She spent part of last night *dreaming* about today's math test.

cycle (sī′kəl) a series of steps that repeat themselves regularly
> *Example:* The *cycle* of seasons includes winter, spring, summer, and fall.

Academic English

theory (thē′ər ē) an unproved explanation based on known facts
> *Example:* My *theory* was that a squirrel was eating all of the birdseed.

relaxed (ri lakst′) at rest rather than tense or worried
> *Example:* Juan felt *relaxed* and calm while he was on vacation.

Answer the questions below. Circle the part of each question that is the answer. The first one has been done for you.

1. Would someone feel more *relaxed* while (on a sandy beach) or at work?
2. Would you describe a *moody* person as predictable or unpredictable?
3. Does the life *cycle* of butterflies change with each butterfly or happen the same way for all butterflies?
4. Would *dreaming* be more likely to occur in a restaurant or in your bed?
5. Would *stages* of life include childhood and adulthood, or running and jumping?
6. As a forest begins to *recover* from a fire, do the plants die or start to grow again?
7. When a scientist has a *theory*, does he or she have an idea or a fear?

 Now skim the article and look for other words that are new to you. Write each new word and its definition in the Personal Dictionary.

While You Read

 Think about why you read. How many hours of sleep do you get each night? As you read, look for sentences that explain why we need to get enough sleep.

Why Is Sleep Good for Us?

1 The human body needs sleep to stay healthy. When people do not sleep well, they can feel more than just tired. Not enough sleep can also make it hard to think clearly. Some people may lack energy. Others may become **moody** and angry if they do not get deep, or heavy, sleep. To find out why the human body
5 needs sleep, scientists study what the body and the brain do during sleep.

Different scientists have different ideas about what sleep does for us, but most scientists believe that there are several reasons that people need to sleep. One **theory,** or idea, is that sleep gives the body and mind time to **recover** from a busy day. Another theory is that the main purpose of sleep is to let the body save energy.

10 Different types of sleep seem to have different effects on the body and mind. Scientists say that we have two types of sleep: quiet sleep and active sleep.

As people fall asleep, they move through the four **stages** of quiet sleep. In the first stage, the muscles loosen and relax, but the mind still knows what is going on around the body. In the second stage, the heart rate, or number of times the heart
15 beats each minute, slows down. Breathing also slows down. The mind is not aware of activity outside the body. In the third and fourth stages, the mind and body keep slowing down, and the muscles are completely **relaxed.** The fourth stage is the deepest, or most relaxed, type of quiet sleep.

During quiet sleep, the body moves through each of the four stages and back
20 again. Then it moves back to the fourth stage. After about 90 minutes of quiet sleep, the body moves into active sleep.

During active sleep, part of the mind is very busy. People sometimes call this type of sleep **dreaming** sleep. Most dreaming takes place during active sleep. Scientists call active sleep REM, or rapid eye movement, sleep. During this kind
25 of sleep, the eyes move back and forth very quickly under the eyelids. The body stays in active sleep for less than 30 minutes. Then it begins the stages of quiet sleep again.

During a night of sleep, the **cycle** of quiet sleep and active sleep repeats itself many times. To feel well rested, a person needs both types of sleep. Many
30 scientists think the two types of sleep help the body in different ways. They believe that quiet sleep gives energy to the body so that people can do their daily tasks well. They believe that active sleep gives energy to the mind so that people can learn and think clearly.

LANGUAGE CONNECTION

Deep sleep means "heavy sleep from which it may be hard to wake up." The word *deep* also means "going far down; not shallow." A lake or hole could be described as deep. What else can be described as deep? Hint: Think of places where you can swim.

CONTENT CONNECTION

In the last paragraph, the second sentence is the topic sentence. It best expresses the main idea of the paragraph. What is the topic sentence in the sixth paragraph? Why do you think it is the topic sentence?

After You Read

A. Organizing Ideas

How are the types of sleep different? Complete the chart below. Write sentences to answer each question for both types of sleep. Use information from the article to help you. Some have been done for you.

Quiet Sleep Versus Active Sleep

Question	Quiet Sleep	Active Sleep
How many stages does this type of sleep have?	Quiet sleep has four stages.	Active sleep has one stage.
What happens to the body during this type of sleep?		
How long does the body stay in this type of sleep?		
What kind of energy does this type of sleep provide?	Quiet sleep gives energy to the body so that it can be active.	
Does dreaming take place during this type of sleep?		
Does this type of sleep occur as soon as a person falls asleep?		

What have you learned about the differences between quiet sleep and active sleep? Write two or more sentences about how the two types of sleep are different. Did the chart help you organize the information in a clear way? Explain your answer.

_____

_____

_____

_____

B. Comprehension Skills

Tip! **Think about how to find answers.** Look back at different parts of the text. What facts help you figure out how to complete the sentences?

Mark box **a, b,** or **c** with an **X** before the choice that best completes each sentence.

Recalling Facts

1. The two types of sleep are
   - ☐ **a.** deep sleep and tired sleep.
   - ☐ **b.** quiet sleep and active sleep.
   - ☐ **c.** dreaming sleep and waking sleep.

2. As people fall asleep, they move through the four stages of
   - ☐ **a.** quiet sleep.
   - ☐ **b.** active sleep.
   - ☐ **c.** dreaming sleep.

3. Scientists also call active sleep
   - ☐ **a.** restless sleep.
   - ☐ **b.** sleepwalking.
   - ☐ **c.** rapid eye movement sleep.

4. Most dreaming occurs
   - ☐ **a.** during quiet sleep.
   - ☐ **b.** during active sleep.
   - ☐ **c.** before falling asleep.

5. The cycle of quiet sleep and active sleep takes place
   - ☐ **a.** once each night.
   - ☐ **b.** three times each night.
   - ☐ **c.** many times each night.

Understanding Ideas

1. Not sleeping well can cause a person to feel
   - ☐ **a.** tired.
   - ☐ **b.** hungry.
   - ☐ **c.** energized.

2. From the article, you can conclude that studying how the body sleeps helps scientists understand why
   - ☐ **a.** people need sleep.
   - ☐ **b.** sleep is often dangerous.
   - ☐ **c.** some people do not need sleep.

3. Quiet sleep and active sleep
   - ☐ **a.** do not give people energy.
   - ☐ **b.** give people energy in the same way.
   - ☐ **c.** give people energy in different ways.

4. A person who had quiet sleep without active sleep for a few nights would probably
   - ☐ **a.** have tired muscles.
   - ☐ **b.** be more rested than usual.
   - ☐ **c.** not be able to learn and think as well as usual.

5. From the article, you can conclude that people need sleep
   - ☐ **a.** more as they get older.
   - ☐ **b.** to think and work well.
   - ☐ **c.** to dream about the future.

C. Reading Strategies

1. Recognizing Words in Context

Find the word *activity* in the article. One definition below is closest to the meaning of that word. One definition has the opposite or nearly the opposite meaning. The remaining definition has a meaning that has nothing to do with the other two words. Label the definitions **C** for *closest,* **O** for *opposite* or *nearly opposite,* and **U** for *unrelated.*

_____ **a.** stillness

_____ **b.** movement

_____ **c.** loudness

2. Distinguishing Fact from Opinion

Two of the statements below present *facts,* which can be proved. The other statement is an *opinion,* which expresses someone's thoughts or beliefs. Label the statements **F** for *fact* and **O** for *opinion.*

_____ **a.** Men who are tired are moodier than women who are tired.

_____ **b.** Dreaming occurs during REM sleep.

_____ **c.** To be fully rested, a person needs both active and quiet sleep.

3. Making Correct Inferences

Two of the statements below are correct *inferences,* or reasonable guesses, that are based on information in the article. The other statement is an incorrect, or faulty, inference. Label the statements **C** for *correct* inference and **I** for *incorrect* inference.

_____ **a.** People spend more time in active sleep than in quiet sleep.

_____ **b.** A person who has trouble paying attention in school may not be getting enough sleep at night.

_____ **c.** Without good sleep, the body's energy levels go down.

4. Understanding Main Ideas

One of the statements below expresses the main idea of the article. Another statement is too general, or too broad. The other explains only part of the article; it is too narrow. Label the statements **M** for *main idea,* **B** for *too broad,* and **N** for *too narrow.*

_____ **a.** People need sleep to stay healthy.

_____ **b.** REM stands for "rapid eye movement."

_____ **c.** People need hours of quiet and active sleep each night to get the energy their bodies and minds need.

5. Responding to the Article

Complete the following sentences in your own words:

One of the things I did best while reading "Why Is Sleep Good for Us?" was

_____

I think that I did this well because _____

D. Expanding Vocabulary

Content-Area Words

Read each item carefully. Write on the line the word or phrase that best completes each sentence.

1. Because my son is moody, I believe that he does not get enough _____.

    food   rapid eye movement   sleep

2. We use sleep to recover the _____ we spend each day working and thinking.

    energy   moods   cycles

3. There are _____ stages of quiet sleep and one stage of active sleep.

    four   three   nine

4. Most dreaming takes place during _____ sleep.

    quiet   active   busy

5. During the night, the cycle of quiet and active sleep is repeated _____ times.

    four   a few   many

Academic English

In the article "Why Is Sleep Good for Us?" you learned that *theory* means "an unproved explanation based on known facts." *Theory* can relate to the ideas scientists have about why people need sleep. *Theory* can also relate to other ideas that explain things, as in the following sentence.

    The mother's theory was that the raw eggs in the cookie dough made her child sick.

Complete the sentence below.

1. Some people have a *theory* that dogs wag their tails when they are _____

Now use the word *theory* in a sentence of your own.

2. _____

You also learned that *relaxed* is an adjective that means "at rest rather than tense or worried." *Relaxed* can also be a verb meaning "rested," as in the following sentence.

    She relaxed on the couch after a long and busy day.

Complete the sentence below.

3. Over summer vacation I *relaxed* by _____

Now use the word *relaxed* in two sentences of your own.

4. _____

5. _____

 Share your new sentences with a partner.

Before You Read

Tip! **Think about what you know.** Skim the article on the opposite page. Look for at least three ways that sedimentary rock can form.

Vocabulary

The content-area and academic English words below appear in "How Sedimentary Rock Forms." Read the definitions and the example sentences.

Content-Area Words

deposits (di poz′its) materials that are left behind, often at the end of a river or stream
    Example: We found gold in the rocky *deposits* at the end of the river.

remains (ri mānz′) materials that are left over, usually after a living thing dies
    Example: My dog found the *remains* of a rabbit in the forest.

formations (fôr mā′shənz) shapes composed of rock or mineral deposits
    Example: The family took pictures of the many rock *formations* in the park.

stalactites (stə lak′fīts) long rocks that hang from the ceiling of a cave
    Example: We looked up at the *stalactites* that hung from the cave ceiling.

stalagmites (stə lag′mīts) long rocks that rise from the floor of a cave
    Example: *Stalagmites* look like tall, thin mountains on the ground of a cave.

Academic English

accumulate (ə kŭ′myə lāt′) to build up or increase in amount
    Example: Homework continued to *accumulate* on my desk while I was sick.

ongoing (on′gō′ing) continuing; not stopping
    Example: Because learning continues all through life, it is an *ongoing* process.

Do any of the words above seem related? Sort the seven vocabulary words into two or more categories. Write the words down on note cards or in a chart. Words may fit into more than one group. You may wish to work with a partner for this activity.

 Now skim the article and look for other words that are new to you. Write each new word and its definition in the Personal Dictionary.

While You Read

 Think about why you read. Have you ever written with chalk? Do you know what chalk is made from? As you read, try to find the answer.

How Sedimentary Rock Forms

1 Sedimentary rock covers about three-fourths of Earth's land surface. It forms when **deposits** of minerals and other materials settle in layers. (Minerals are natural substances usually found in the ground.) These layers are called strata. People can see strata clearly in rock walls, such as those in the Grand Canyon in Arizona.

5 Earth has many kinds of sedimentary rock. Each kind forms in a different way. Some sedimentary rocks form as wind and water leave behind small bits of rock and sand. Others form from chemicals or from the **remains** of living things.

The most common kinds of sedimentary rock come from deposits left behind by water. The water wears away rocks—carrying away, and then leaving behind, 10 sand and small bits of rock. Over time the deposits pile up into layers. Over thousands of years, new layers cover up old layers. The weight of the layers presses the bits of rock together. Water seeps, or moves slowly, through the layers and leaves behind minerals. These minerals glue the bits together.

Some sedimentary materials are formed by either water, wind, or large moving 15 sheets of ice called glaciers. Sandstone is rock made from grains of sand left behind by water. People can see huge sandstone **formations** in Monument Valley in Arizona. Loess is a crumbly, or easily broken, sedimentary material. It comes from dust and dirt blown by the wind and is a yellowish-brown color. Loess covers large areas of the world. Tillite is a sedimentary material made up of clay, 20 large rocks, and other minerals pressed together. Moving glaciers form tillite.

Most kinds of sedimentary rock are formed from the minerals that **accumulate** in water over time. As the water flows, it leaves these minerals behind in different places. **Stalactites** and **stalagmites** are examples of rock formed in this way. They are found in dark openings in Earth's surface, called caves. Travertine is another 25 rock of this type. It is formed by hot springs, or hot streams of water that flow right out of the ground. People can see travertine formations at Mammoth Hot Springs in Yellowstone National Park. These formations are made up of large, flat pieces sitting on top of each other like an uneven stack of trays.

Sedimentary rock can also come from the remains of living things. Chalk and 30 coal are two kinds of rock that form this way. Chalk comes from animal skeletons and shells that gather on the bottom, or floor, of the sea. Coal comes from the remains of plants. Over time, the layers of animal and plant remains become solid chalk and coal. All sedimentary rock takes a long time to form. The **ongoing** process can take thousands or even millions of years.

LANGUAGE CONNECTION

Sedimentary rock comes from mineral deposits. People also use the word *deposit* when they put money into a bank. Have you ever made a deposit at a bank?

CONTENT CONNECTION

The letter *c* in the word *stalactite* can remind you that stalactites hang from the *ceiling* of a cave. The letter *g* in the word *stalagmite* can remind you that stalagmites rise up from the *ground* of a cave. Can you think of a way to remember what travertine is?

After You Read

A. Organizing Ideas

How does sedimentary rock form? Complete the chart below. In each box, complete the first sentence to describe one way that sedimentary rock can form. Then write sentences to explain how sedimentary rock forms that way. The first box has been done for you.

How Sedimentary Rock Forms

Sedimentary rock can be formed from water deposits.

Water erodes rocks and carries away small pieces of them. These pieces are called deposits. Deposits pile up into layers over time. The layers press together over thousands of years. Minerals glue the layers together, and a type of sedimentary rock forms.

Sedimentary materials can be formed by _____

_____

_____

_____

Sedimentary rock can be formed from _____

_____

_____

_____

How did this chart help you organize your information about sedimentary rock? Write two or more sentences about one way that sedimentary rock can form. Do you think this type of chart is a useful way to help you learn? Explain your answer.

_____

_____

_____

B. Comprehension Skills

 Think about how to find answers. Look back at what you read. The information is in the text, but you may have to look in several sentences to find it.

Mark box **a, b,** or **c** with an **X** before the choice that best completes each sentence.

Recalling Facts

1. The most common kinds of sedimentary rock come from deposits left by
   - ☐ **a.** wind.
   - ☐ **b.** water.
   - ☐ **c.** plants.

2. Stalactites and stalagmites are examples of rock formed by
   - ☐ **a.** wind.
   - ☐ **b.** water.
   - ☐ **c.** the Sun.

3. Chalk and coal are sedimentary rocks that come from
   - ☐ **a.** sand.
   - ☐ **b.** gemstones.
   - ☐ **c.** the remains of living things.

4. Sedimentary rock forms
   - ☐ **a.** overnight.
   - ☐ **b.** over 10 to 20 years.
   - ☐ **c.** over thousands of years.

5. Sedimentary rock covers
   - ☐ **a.** a small part of Earth's surface.
   - ☐ **b.** about one-third of Earth's surface.
   - ☐ **c.** about three-fourths of Earth's surface.

Understanding Ideas

1. From the article, you can conclude that sedimentary rock forms from minerals deposited
   - ☐ **a.** in layers.
   - ☐ **b.** in tall piles.
   - ☐ **c.** into deep holes.

2. Sedimentary rocks such as sandstone, travertine, and coal form
   - ☐ **a.** in the same way.
   - ☐ **b.** in different ways.
   - ☐ **c.** from the same materials.

3. Most sedimentary rocks are composed of minerals
   - ☐ **a.** found in caves.
   - ☐ **b.** that come from lava.
   - ☐ **c.** that used to be part of other rocks.

4. From the article, you can conclude that sedimentary rock formations can
   - ☐ **a.** be seen mainly underwater.
   - ☐ **b.** be seen in many different kinds of places.
   - ☐ **c.** no longer be seen in most parts of the world.

5. You can also conclude that all types of sedimentary rock form from
   - ☐ **a.** the force of the wind.
   - ☐ **b.** exactly the same materials.
   - ☐ **c.** layers of matter left behind over time.

C. Reading Strategies

1. Recognizing Words in Context

Find the word *common* in the article. One definition below is closest to the meaning of that word. One definition has the opposite or nearly the opposite meaning. The remaining definition has a meaning that has nothing to do with the other two words. Label the definitions **C** for *closest*, **O** for *opposite* or *nearly opposite*, and **U** for *unrelated*.

_____ **a.** unusual

_____ **b.** often seen

_____ **c.** cold

2. Distinguishing Fact from Opinion

Two of the statements below present *facts*, which can be proved. The other statement is an *opinion*, which expresses someone's thoughts or beliefs. Label the statements **F** for *fact* and **O** for *opinion*.

_____ **a.** Sandstone forms when sand is left behind by water.

_____ **b.** One kind of sedimentary rock that forms from dead things is coal.

_____ **c.** The Grand Canyon is the best place to see sedimentary rock.

3. Making Correct Inferences

Two of the statements below are correct *inferences*, or reasonable guesses, that are based on information in the article. The other statement is an incorrect, or faulty, inference. Label the statements **C** for *correct* inference and **I** for *incorrect* inference.

_____ **a.** Without water, stalagmites and stalactites would not form in caves.

_____ **b.** The minerals in sedimentary rock are very old.

_____ **c.** Coal and chalk form more quickly than other types of sedimentary rock.

4. Understanding Main Ideas

One of the statements below expresses the main idea of the article. Another statement is too general, or too broad. The other explains only part of the article; it is too narrow. Label the statements **M** for *main idea*, **B** for *too broad*, and **N** for *too narrow*.

_____ **a.** Sedimentary material comes from many minerals.

_____ **b.** Tillite forms from minerals that are pressed together, but loess forms from dust blown by the wind.

_____ **c.** Sedimentary material comes from different places and can form many types of sedimentary rock.

5. Responding to the Article

Complete the following sentence in your own words:

What interested me most about "How Sedimentary Rock Forms" is

_____

_____

D. Expanding Vocabulary

Content-Area Words

Complete each sentence with a word from the box. Write the missing word on the line.

| deposits | remains | formations | stalactites | stalagmites |

1. We saw _____ hanging down from the ceiling in the cave.

2. Water can leave behind _____ such as sand and bits of rock.

3. When plants die, their _____ can turn into coal after many years.

4. _____ are piles of minerals sticking up from the floor of a cave.

5. People can see huge rock _____ made of sandstone in Arizona.

Academic English

In the article "How Sedimentary Rock Forms," you learned that *accumulate* means "to build up or increase in amount." *Accumulate* can relate to how minerals build up in water that runs over rocks. *Accumulate* can also mean "to collect or gain more of something," as in the following sentence.

I hope to accumulate many books over the years.

Complete the sentence below.

1. When teachers collect assignments and tests, they *accumulate* a great deal of _____

Now use the word *accumulate* in a sentence of your own.

2. _____

_____

You also learned that *ongoing* means "continuing" or "not stopping." *Ongoing* can relate to natural processes, such as how minerals build up in layers to make sedimentary rock. *Ongoing* can also relate to other continuing actions, as in the following sentence.

Cleaning the attic is an ongoing project.

Complete the sentence below.

3. The *ongoing* improvements to the house included a new kitchen and _____

Now use the word *ongoing* in two sentences of your own.

4. _____

5. _____

 Share your new sentences with a partner.

Vocabulary Assessment

Reading a Newspaper Advertisement

Read the advertisement. Circle the word that completes each sentence.

Explore the New Dinosaur Museum!

Visit our city's newest museum. Learn how dinosaurs lived and why they became extinct.

- Look at lifelike statues that (**simulate, recover**) how real dinosaurs may have looked and sounded.

- Watch as paleontologists study dinosaur (**remains, deposits**) that were discovered in Australia and brought to America. Scientists have found dinosaur fossils in many (**stages, regions**) of Earth.

Visit our museum and decide for yourself!

- See the interesting physical (**ecosystem, features**) of different dinosaurs. You won't forget their sharp claws and teeth, pointed horns, spiked tails, and long wings.

- Find out why dinosaurs became extinct. Some scientists believe that (**fertile, ongoing**) changes in dinosaurs' environments caused them to die out slowly. Others believe that the dinosaurs died suddenly.

Reading an Instant-Messaging Conversation

Read the instant-messaging conversation between Ronak and Sara. Then complete the sentences. Use words from the Word Bank.

Word Bank

relaxed   undergo
encounter   formations
pincers

INSTA-CHAT

Ronak: Hello, Sara. Are you online?

Sara: Hi, Ronak. I was just reading an article about scuba diving on the Internet. I am really excited about our trip to Australia!

Ronak: I am excited too. I am also scared! I've never been scuba diving before.

Sara: Try not to worry. We have to _____ many days of scuba diving lessons before we really start exploring. I am looking forward to the feeling of weightlessness when I am underwater. I'll feel so _____!

Ronak: I'm still scared. Will we _____ any dangerous underwater animals while we dive? My uncle is a scuba diver, and he told me that a lobster pinched him with its sharp _____ once.

Sara: Relax! Aren't you curious about the underwater rock _____?

Ronak: Sure, I want to see how great they look . . . but I'm still a bit nervous.

Sara: I think it's all right to be a little bit nervous. We're going to have a great time, though! Bye, Ronak! ;)

Work with a partner. Talk about what the words mean. How can you use the words to talk about a wolf? List your ideas in the outline of the wolves below.

destroyed	accumulate	prey	erosion	protein
theory	restore	cycle	mission	abdomen

Use all of the words above in a paragraph of your own. Each sentence may include one or more of the words. To help you start writing, look at the ideas you wrote about. After you write your sentences, read them over. If you find a mistake, correct it.

_____

_____

_____

_____

_____

_____

_____

_____

_____

_____

Before You Read

 Think about what you know. Read the title and the first sentence of the article on the opposite page. What types of animals and plants would you expect to see at the seashore?

Vocabulary

The content-area and academic English words below appear in "Surviving the Tides." Read the definitions and the example sentences.

Content-Area Words

seashore (sē′shôr′) land near or on the edge of the sea
> *Example:* We ate our picnic lunch near the water on the sandy *seashore*.

tides (tīdz) the rise and fall of water levels that, in most oceans, takes place twice each day
> *Example:* High *tides* push the water onto the beach early in the morning and late at night.

environment (en vī′rən mənt) the surroundings of a plant or animal that affect its life
> *Example:* A fish cannot survive in a dry *environment*.

suction cup (suk′shən kup) a cup-shaped object that sticks to a flat surface through lowered air pressure
> *Example:* The *suction cup* on the back of the hook holds it to the wall.

receding (ri sēd′ing) moving back or away
> *Example:* The *receding* floodwater returned to the river.

Academic English

challenge (chal′inj) something that is difficult to do
> *Example:* His *challenge* was to move the heavy refrigerator into the truck.

eventually (i ven′choo ə lē) at a later time
> *Example:* It is cloudy outside, so I think it will rain *eventually*.

Read again the example sentences that follow the content-area and academic English word definitions. With a partner, discuss the meanings of the words and sentences. Then make up a sentence of your own for each word. Your teacher may wish to discuss your new sentences in class.

 Now skim the article and look for other words that are new to you. Write each new word and its definition in the Personal Dictionary.

While You Read

 Think about why you read. Have you ever heard of a tide pool? As you read, try to find information about how tide pools help sea life survive the tides.

Surviving the TIDES

1 For the animals and plants living at the **seashore,** each day is a **challenge.** The seashore provides many places to live. It has large rocks and sand dunes, or large hills of sand. Of course, it also has the open ocean. The movement of the **tides** makes the seashore a place that changes all the time. Sea plants and animals

5 that are covered by water in the morning may be left in dry sand under the heat of the sun by afternoon. How can living things survive in this difficult **environment?**

In most oceans, the tide reaches its farthest point up the shore about every 12 hours. This is high tide, during which most of the beach is usually under water. Some forms of sea life, or sea animals and plants, hang on tightly to rocks, so

10 the strong waves do not move them all to the shore. A sea snail uses its foot like a **suction cup** to hang on to rocks. Hard-shelled sea animals called barnacles produce a liquid that allows their shells to stick to rock. Instead of roots like a plant's, seaweed has a part called a holdfast. The holdfast attaches to rocks or to the bottom of the sea.

15 These forms of sea life work hard not to let the waves carry them to shore, but they do not always succeed. As the water level goes down with the **receding** tide, some sea life is left behind on the shore. Sea urchins, sea stars, and seaweed are a few of the living things that may **eventually** die if they are left on the shore without water. Other sea life may survive in small pools, or puddles, of water left

20 behind by the receding tide. These small pools, called tide pools, are homes for many sea plants and animals, including seaweed, sea anemones, sea stars, crabs, and clams. Each day, these creatures struggle to stay alive in the pools before the next high tide.

At high tide, cool water fills the tide pools. The ocean water is full of oxygen

25 and tiny creatures called plankton. Some animals, such as barnacles, eat the tiny plankton. At low tide, the creatures are in danger of using up all the oxygen and food in the pool. Also, the water in the pool gets warm and begins to dry up. Some creatures do not survive. Animals such as sea anemones and clams close up their bodies or shells to keep water in. Some seaweed produces mucus, a substance

30 that helps to keep it moist, or slightly wet. When the waves finally reach high tide again, they fill the pools with cool seawater. This may seem like a moment of relief. However, it is really just the beginning of a new challenge. Now the sea creatures must avoid being carried to shore by the waves.

LANGUAGE CONNECTION

A hyphen can connect two words that describe something. In the phrase *hard-shelled sea animals*, *hard* describes the sea animals' shells. *Hard-shelled* describes the sea animals. In your own words, tell what a *long-haired cat* is.

CONTENT CONNECTION

Some seaweed produces mucus for moisture. What other form of sea life in this article produces a liquid to help itself survive?

After You Read

A. Organizing Ideas

How do high and low tides affect sea life? Complete the cause-and-effect chart below. Write sentences about the effects that high and low tides have on sea life. Use the article to help you.

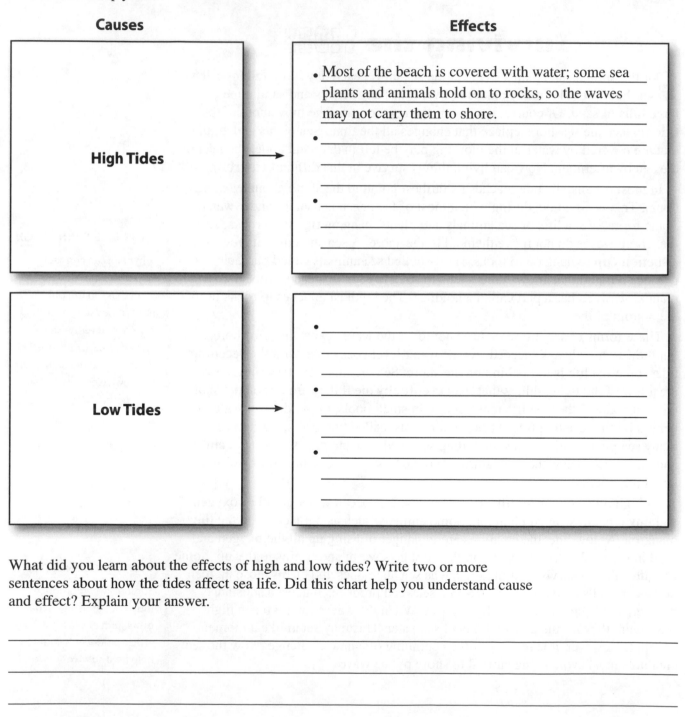

Causes

Effects

High Tides →

- Most of the beach is covered with water; some sea plants and animals hold on to rocks, so the waves may not carry them to shore.
- _____
- _____

Low Tides →

- _____
- _____
- _____

What did you learn about the effects of high and low tides? Write two or more sentences about how the tides affect sea life. Did this chart help you understand cause and effect? Explain your answer.

_____

_____

_____

B. Comprehension Skills

Tip! **Think about how to find answers.** Think about what each sentence means. Try to say it to yourself in your own words before you complete it.

Mark box **a, b,** or **c** with an **X** before the choice that best completes each sentence.

Recalling Facts

1. At high tide, some kinds of sea life hold on to rocks, so they do not get
   - ☐ **a.** eaten by fish.
   - ☐ **b.** covered by water.
   - ☐ **c.** carried to shore by waves.

2. As water in a tide pool dries up, sea anemones and clams close up, so they do not
   - ☐ **a.** drown.
   - ☐ **b.** get cold.
   - ☐ **c.** lose water.

3. Some seaweed produces mucus that helps to
   - ☐ **a.** keep the seaweed moist.
   - ☐ **b.** keep flies off the seaweed.
   - ☐ **c.** keep waves from hitting the seaweed.

4. While waiting for high tide, creatures in a tide pool are in danger of
   - ☐ **a.** drowning.
   - ☐ **b.** getting cold.
   - ☐ **c.** using up all the food in the pool.

5. Cool seawater pours into tide pools at
   - ☐ **a.** low tide.
   - ☐ **b.** high tide.
   - ☐ **c.** all times of the day.

Understanding Ideas

1. From the article, you can conclude that most high tides occur about
   - ☐ **a.** every hour.
   - ☐ **b.** twice each day.
   - ☐ **c.** once each week.

2. The article suggests that at high tide some forms of sea life struggle to
   - ☐ **a.** get enough oxygen.
   - ☐ **b.** stay above water level.
   - ☐ **c.** avoid being washed up on shore.

3. The article also suggests that at low tide sea life in tide pools cannot always
   - ☐ **a.** get enough food and moisture.
   - ☐ **b.** escape large creatures like sharks.
   - ☐ **c.** protect itself from crashing waves.

4. Sea creatures at the seashore work hard to survive in
   - ☐ **a.** bad weather.
   - ☐ **b.** changing conditions.
   - ☐ **c.** a polluted environment.

5. From the article, you can conclude that the animals likely to survive in tide pools can
   - ☐ **a.** get oxygen from the air.
   - ☐ **b.** live only on seaweed.
   - ☐ **c.** live in shallow water for hours at a time.

C. Reading Strategies

1. Recognizing Words in Context

Find the word *avoid* in the article. One definition below is closest to the meaning of that word. One definition has the opposite or nearly the opposite meaning. The remaining definition has a meaning that has nothing to do with the other two words. Label the definitions **C** for *closest*, **O** for *opposite* or *nearly opposite*, and **U** for *unrelated*.

_____ **a.** get close to

_____ **b.** turn quickly

_____ **c.** stay away from

2. Distinguishing Fact from Opinion

Two of the statements below present *facts*, which can be proved. The other statement is an *opinion*, which expresses someone's thoughts or beliefs. Label the statements **F** for *fact* and **O** for *opinion*.

_____ **a.** During low tide, some sea life is left on shore when the water level goes down.

_____ **b.** The most interesting animals in the world live at the seashore.

_____ **c.** Some sea creatures that hang on to rocks are not carried to shore by the waves.

3. Making Correct Inferences

Two of the statements below are correct *inferences,* or reasonable guesses, that are based on information in the article. The other statement is an incorrect, or faulty, inference. Label the statements **C** for *correct* inference and **I** for *incorrect* inference.

_____ **a.** Low tide can be dangerous for creatures living at the seashore.

_____ **b.** Barnacles need oxygen and plankton in order to survive.

_____ **c.** After high tide, sea creatures are safe for several days.

4. Understanding Main Ideas

One of the statements below expresses the main idea of the article. Another statement is too general, or too broad. The other explains only part of the article; it is too narrow. Label the statements **M** for *main idea,* **B** for *too broad,* and **N** for *too narrow.*

_____ **a.** Sea creatures struggle to survive the changing tides of the seashore.

_____ **b.** Sea urchins may die if they are left on shore without water at low tide.

_____ **c.** High and low tides make it hard for sea life to survive.

5. Responding to the Article

Complete the following sentence in your own words:

By reading "Surviving the Tides," I learned

_____

_____

D. Expanding Vocabulary

Content-Area Words

Cross out one word or phrase in each row that is not related to the word in dark type.

1. **seashore**	environment	tides	desert	ocean
2. **tides**	high	low	receding	boat
3. **environment**	world	beginning	seashore	living things
4. **suction cup**	loose	stick	sea snail	rocks
5. **receding**	tides	low	moving back	moving forward

Academic English

In the article "Surviving the Tides," you learned that *challenge* is a noun that means "something that is difficult to do." *Challenge* can also be a verb that means "to dare someone to do something difficult," as in the following sentence.

I would like to challenge you to stay underwater for two minutes.

Complete the sentence below.

1. If you *challenge* someone to a swimming race, you will need to swim _____

Now use the word *challenge* in a sentence of your own.

2. _____

_____

You also learned that *eventually* means "at a later time." *Eventually* can describe how sea creatures will die at a later time if they are out of the water for too long. *Eventually* can also describe other things that will happen at a later time, as in the following sentence.

You will eventually get hungry if you do not eat.

Complete the sentence below.

3. It will *eventually* become dark outside after the sun _____

Now use the word *eventually* in two sentences of your own.

4. _____

5. _____

 Share your new sentences with a partner.

The Camera: Amazing Invention

Before You Read

 **Think about what you know.** Read the lesson title above. What kinds of cameras have you used?

_____

Vocabulary

The content-area and academic English words below appear in "The Camera: Amazing Invention." Read the definitions and the example sentences.

Content-Area Words

projects (prə jekts′) causes a shadow, light, or image to appear on a surface
Example: A camera *projects* a movie onto a large screen in the movie theater.

enclosed (en klōzd′) surrounded on all sides
Example: Our yard is *enclosed* by a fence so that our dog cannot get out.

record (ri kôrd′) to set down on paper
Example: Teachers *record* the grades of each student during the year.

exposed (iks pōzd′) allowed to have light shine on it
Example: The red color of the couch faded to pink after it was *exposed* to years of sunlight.

instant (in′stənt) ready very quickly
Example: Mix *instant* soup mix with hot water, and it is ready to eat.

Academic English

error (er′ər) a mistake
Example: I made only one *error* on the math test.

reversed (ri vurst′) changed to the opposite
Example: We planned to run first and stretch afterwards, but then the order was *reversed*.

Complete the sentences below that contain the content-area and academic English words above. Use the spaces provided. The first one has been done for you.

1. The computer *projects* the graph by showing the graph's image on a wall_____.

2. I asked for an *instant* reply to my letter because _____.

3. The field was *enclosed* by _____.

4. Our *error* was that we turned right when we should have _____.

5. Mario's shirt was *reversed* so that its front was _____.

6. Sarah likes to *record* what she does each day by _____.

7. Some animals do not like to be *exposed* to light because _____.

_____

Dictionary Now skim the article and look for other words that are new to you. Write each new word and its definition in the Personal Dictionary.

While You Read

 Think about why you read. Have you ever received negatives when your film was developed from a camera? As you read, look for the paragraph about the first negative.

The Camera
Amazing Invention

1 Ideas for useful inventions often take a lot of work and time to create. The camera took a long time to go from an idea to an invention. A camera works because of an idea, or concept, that a Chinese scholar first described more than 2,000 years ago. Later, Greek and Arab scholars also understood the concept.
5 This concept is that during daytime, a tiny hole in the wall of an unlighted room without windows **projects** an image from outside into the room.

About 500 years ago, people used this concept to make an **enclosed** area with an opening that let in a beam, or straight line, of light. Artists used this area, called the *camera obscura,* to project images, or pictures, onto paper. Then they traced
10 and painted the images. The enclosed area worked like a camera does. However, it did not **record** an image automatically, or by itself.

In the early 1800s, a man named Thomas Wedgwood spread a chemical that contained silver on a sheet of paper. He saw that the paper could record an image when he **exposed** it to light. But Wedgwood also saw that it got darker and darker
15 as the light kept shining on it. That showed that this paper was light-sensitive, or affected by changes in light. A French inventor named Joseph Niépce used a similar idea to make a paper to use in the camera obscura. Niépce was able to make a black-and-white image with his light-sensitive paper. With the use of a chemical that contained acid, he was also able to keep the image from turning black. He found an
20 **error,** though. The parts of the image that should have looked white looked black. The parts of the image that should have looked black looked white. The black areas and the white areas were **reversed.** Niépce had made the first negative.

Niépce began to work on a second way to record images. In 1826 he used light-sensitive chemicals on a flat metal surface called a plate. Then he exposed the plate in
25 a camera obscura all day. This faint, or hard-to-see, image was the first photograph.

Niépce shared his work with a French artist and inventor named Louis Daguerre. Daguerre then used a new mixture of chemicals on the metal plate. A clear image called a daguerreotype formed on the plate in 30 minutes. After this invention, the first camera was sold in 1839. However, it still took hard work, and
30 many chemicals and devices, to create a photograph.

George Eastman invented the Kodak camera in 1888. This camera was the first one that was easy to use and that required no chemicals. It used rolls of film like some we use today. Now **instant** cameras and digital cameras can give us photos right away.

LANGUAGE CONNECTION

The prefix *un-* means "not," so *unlighted* means "not lighted." Can you think of another word that begins with the prefix *un-?*

CONTENT CONNECTION

Thomas Wedgwood and Joseph Niépce used chemicals, such as silver nitrate, to record images on paper. Can you think of things we use in our daily lives that contain chemicals?

After You Read

A. Organizing Ideas

What do you know or want to know about how the camera was invented?
Complete the K-W-L chart below. List four things you know, four things you want to learn about, and four facts you have learned from the article about how the camera was invented. Some parts have been done for you.

What I Know	What I Want to Know	What I Have Learned
People worked for many years to invent cameras like the kinds we use today.		
		People who used early cameras needed different chemicals to take pictures. Now we can use film or digital cameras.
Many people helped to invent and improve the camera.		
	When could people first buy their own cameras?	The first camera was sold in 1839. However, cameras that were easy to use were not available until George Eastman invented the Kodak camera in 1888.

As you completed this chart, did you learn more about something that you already knew? Write two or more sentences about something that you have learned about the way the camera was invented. Would you use a chart like this again? Why or why not?

_____

_____

_____

_____

B. Comprehension Skills

Tip! **Think about how to find answers.** Read each sentence below. Underline the words that will help you figure out how to complete each item.

Mark box **a, b,** or **c** with an **X** before the choice that best completes each sentence.

Recalling Facts

1. The first photograph was made in 1826 by
   - ☐ **a.** Joseph Niépce.
   - ☐ **b.** Greek scholars.
   - ☐ **c.** George Eastman.

2. When Louis Daguerre put his mixture of chemicals on a metal plate, an image formed
   - ☐ **a.** instantly.
   - ☐ **b.** in 24 hours.
   - ☐ **c.** in 30 minutes.

3. George Eastman invented the Kodak camera, which was the first
   - ☐ **a.** camera.
   - ☐ **b.** easy-to-use camera.
   - ☐ **c.** camera sold to the public.

4. Pictures became available right away with the invention of
   - ☐ **a.** lenses.
   - ☐ **b.** metal plates.
   - ☐ **c.** instant and digital cameras.

5. An enclosed area that worked like a camera does but could not automatically record an image was the
   - ☐ **a.** Kodak camera.
   - ☐ **b.** daguerreotype.
   - ☐ **c.** camera obscura.

Understanding Ideas

1. From the article, you can conclude that a problem with Niépce's first camera was the
   - ☐ **a.** amount of film used on one image.
   - ☐ **b.** length of time it took for an image to form.
   - ☐ **c.** large number of people needed to work the camera.

2. According to the article, light-sensitive papers and metal plates were needed to
   - ☐ **a.** measure temperature.
   - ☐ **b.** record images in a camera.
   - ☐ **c.** create enough light for picture-taking.

3. The invention of the camera is the result of
   - ☐ **a.** an accident.
   - ☐ **b.** the ideas of one person.
   - ☐ **c.** the work of many people over time.

4. From the article, you can conclude that a problem with the camera obscura was that it had
   - ☐ **a.** no lens.
   - ☐ **b.** no way to project images.
   - ☐ **c.** no way to record an image automatically.

5. You can also conclude that people did not have to use chemicals to take pictures after the invention of
   - ☐ **a.** the Kodak camera.
   - ☐ **b.** coated metal plates.
   - ☐ **c.** the camera obscura.

C. Reading Strategies

1. Recognizing Words in Context

Find the word *flat* in the article. One definition below is closest to the meaning of that word. One definition has the opposite or nearly the opposite meaning. The remaining definition has a meaning that has nothing to do with the other two words. Label the definitions **C** for *closest*, **O** for *opposite* or *nearly opposite*, and **U** for *unrelated*.

_____ **a.** smooth

_____ **b.** bumpy

_____ **c.** wet

2. Distinguishing Fact from Opinion

Two of the statements below present *facts*, which can be proved. The other statement is an *opinion*, which expresses someone's thoughts or beliefs. Label the statements **F** for *fact* and **O** for *opinion*.

_____ **a.** Joseph Niépce did the most important work with cameras.

_____ **b.** The camera obscura was a tool used by artists.

_____ **c.** A daguerreotype is a clear image that forms on a metal plate.

3. Making Correct Inferences

Two of the statements below are correct *inferences*, or reasonable guesses, that are based on information in the article. The other statement is an incorrect, or faulty, inference. Label the statements **C** for *correct* inference and **I** for *incorrect* inference.

_____ **a.** After the invention of the daguerreotype, people could make and sell cameras.

_____ **b.** The concept of a camera as we know it today has been known for many thousands of years.

_____ **c.** People liked George Eastman's Kodak camera because it was easier to use than earlier cameras.

4. Understanding Main Ideas

One of the statements below expresses the main idea of the article. Another statement is too general, or too broad. The other explains only part of the article; it is too narrow. Label the statements **M** for *main idea*, **B** for *too broad*, and **N** for *too narrow*.

_____ **a.** Joseph Niépce invented the first negative.

_____ **b.** The camera is a very useful invention.

_____ **c.** Many people helped to invent today's cameras by thinking of new ideas over time.

5. Responding to the Article

Complete the following sentence in your own words:

Before reading "The Camera: Amazing Invention," I already knew

_____

_____

D. Expanding Vocabulary

Content-Area Words

Read each item carefully. Write on the line the word or phrase that best completes each sentence.

1. The _____ projected an image onto paper so that an artist could paint it.
   daguerreotype   digital camera   camera obscura

2. Thomas Wedgwood saw that _____ paper could record an image.
   heat-sensitive   light-sensitive   pressure-sensitive

3. Niépce made the first photograph when he exposed a _____ in a camera obscura all day.
   plate   bowl   cup

4. Instant cameras and _____ cameras make it easy to take pictures today.
   daguerreotype   darker   digital

5. A camera obscura was an enclosed area with a hole that let in _____.
   chemicals   light   film

Academic English

In the article "The Camera: Amazing Invention," you learned that *error* means "a mistake." *Error* can also mean "the condition of being mistaken," as in the following sentence.

We were in error when we thought the sky was yellow.

Complete the sentence below.

1. She said that the show started at noon, but she was in *error* because _____

Now use the word *error* in a sentence of your own.

2. _____

You also learned that *reversed* means "changed to the opposite." *Reversed* can also mean "caused something to change to the opposite," as in the following sentence.

I was driving the wrong way, so I reversed the direction of my car.

Complete the sentence below.

3. The baseball umpire *reversed* his call after he realized that he was _____

Now use the word *reversed* in two sentences of your own.

4. _____

5. _____

 Share your new sentences with a partner.

Before You Read

 Think about what you know. Read the lesson title above. What do you predict the article will be about? What do you already know about simple and compound machines?

Vocabulary

The content-area and academic English words below appear in "Machines: Simple and Compound." Read the definitions and the example sentences.

Content-Area Words

claw (klô) sharp, curved object that can hold or grab something
Example: The lobster held a piece of food in its big *claw*.

inclined plane (in klīnd′ plān) a flat, tilted surface
Example: People use an *inclined plane* to slide heavy furniture up into trucks.

shovel (shuv′əl) a tool with a blade and a long handle that can be used to pick up and move dirt
Example: I used a *shovel* to dig a hole so that I could plant a tree.

gears (gērz) wheels connected at the edges with teeth
Example: The *gears* helped to turn the factory machine.

systems (sis′təmz) groups of parts that work together
Example: Many houses have *systems* that heat and cool the rooms.

Academic English

compound (kom′pound′) made of more than one part
Example: A *compound* word is made of two words put together.

task (task) a job or piece of work
Example: My favorite cleaning *task* is to sweep the floor.

Do any of the words above seem related? Sort the seven vocabulary words into two or more categories. Write the words down on note cards or in a chart. Words may fit into more than one group. You may wish to work with a partner for this activity.

 Now skim the article and look for other words that are new to you. Write each new word and its definition in the Personal Dictionary.

While You Read

 Think about why you read. What simple and compound machines have you used? As you read, think about the machines you use each day.

Machines: Simple and Compound

1 A machine is a device that helps people do work. In science, people use the word *work* to describe what happens when a force, or power, acts on an object to move it. For example, carpenters (people who build things with wood) do work when they pull nails out of wood. Movers do work when they put boxes 5 into a truck. They use simple machines to do these jobs.

Machines make it easier for people to do work. This is because a person who uses machines does not need to use as much force to move an object. A person who uses the **claw** end of a hammer to pull nails out of wood uses less force than a person who pulls the nails out with his or her fingers. A person who pushes 10 a heavy box up a ramp (a flat, tilted surface) into a truck uses less force than a person who lifts the heavy box into the truck.

The hammer and the ramp are examples of two types of simple machines, or machines with very few parts. The hammer is an example of a lever, a bar that moves force from one place, or point, to another while turning on a third point. A 15 ramp is an example of a type of simple machine called an **inclined plane.** Levers and inclined planes are not the only types of simple machines. Wedges, screws, wheels and axles, and pulleys are also types of simple machines.

When someone uses two or more simple machines together, the new machine is called a **compound** machine. For example, a **shovel** is made up of two simple 20 machines, the wedge and the lever. The part of the shovel that can break into and hold material, such as dirt, is the wedge. The handle, or the part of the shovel that a person holds, is the lever.

A bike is a compound machine that uses many different simple machines. The brake handles that you squeeze to stop your bike are levers. A small metal 25 piece called a screw connects the handlebars with the front wheel for steering, or turning, the bike. The wheels, the circular **gears,** and the pedals you push with your feet are all wheel-and-axle **systems.** These systems work together so that you need to use only a little force to make the bike move.

Imagine what would happen if you tried to break up ground for a garden 30 without the wedge or lever of a shovel. What would happen if you tried to ride a bike without pedals or gears? Either of these would be a difficult **task** without machines. Simple machines make tasks easier to do. When simple machines are put together to make compound machines, work becomes even easier.

CONTENT CONNECTION

Can you think of a time when you used a hammer or a ramp? What would you have done instead if you had not used the hammer or the ramp?

LANGUAGE CONNECTION

Handlebars is a word made up of two other words. Can you think of other compound words? Hint: Where can you read about current events?

After You Read

A. Organizing Ideas

What are the different kinds of machines? Complete the chart below. Under each kind of machine, write down its definition. Then list at least three examples of each kind of machine. Use the article to help you. Some have been done for you.

	Simple Machines	Compound Machines
Definition		
Examples	lever (such as a hammer)	shovel

What kind of work can you do with simple and compound machines? Write two or more sentences to answer this question. Did the chart help you understand the different kinds of machines? Would you use this kind of chart again?

_____

_____

_____

_____

_____

_____

B. Comprehension Skills

 Think about how to find answers. Look back at what you read. The information is in the text, but you may have to look in several sentences to find it.

Mark box **a, b,** or **c** with an **X** before the choice that best completes each sentence.

Recalling Facts

1. Two or more simple machines joined together make a
   - ☐ **a.** lever.
   - ☐ **b.** screw.
   - ☐ **c.** compound machine.

2. Levers, inclined planes, wedges, screws, wheels and axles, and pulleys are types of
   - ☐ **a.** ramps.
   - ☐ **b.** simple machines.
   - ☐ **c.** compound machines.

3. A compound machine that is made up of a lever and a wedge is
   - ☐ **a.** a shovel.
   - ☐ **b.** a hammer.
   - ☐ **c.** a wheelbarrow.

4. When a person uses a machine, work becomes
   - ☐ **a.** easier.
   - ☐ **b.** more difficult.
   - ☐ **c.** more important.

5. The number of simple machine types is
   - ☐ **a.** six.
   - ☐ **b.** one.
   - ☐ **c.** twelve.

Understanding Ideas

1. A seesaw on a playground is an example of a
   - ☐ **a.** lever.
   - ☐ **b.** wedge.
   - ☐ **c.** wheel and axle.

2. A flat, tilted board that can be used when walking from a beach to the deck of a ship is an example of a
   - ☐ **a.** simple machine.
   - ☐ **b.** complex machine.
   - ☐ **c.** compound machine.

3. When you use a compound machine instead of a simple machine, your work is
   - ☐ **a.** harder to do.
   - ☐ **b.** easier to do.
   - ☐ **c.** equally difficult to do.

4. Machines make work easier to do because they
   - ☐ **a.** let people use less force.
   - ☐ **b.** are better at work than people are.
   - ☐ **c.** can do work without any help from people.

5. One compound machine with screws, levers, and wheel-and-axle systems is
   - ☐ **a.** an ax.
   - ☐ **b.** a bike.
   - ☐ **c.** a wheelbarrow.

C. Reading Strategies

1. Recognizing Words in Context

Find the word *simple* in the article. One definition below is closest to the meaning of that word. One definition has the opposite or nearly the opposite meaning. The remaining definition has a meaning that has nothing to do with the other two words. Label the definitions **C** for *closest,* **O** for *opposite* or *nearly opposite,* and **U** for *unrelated.*

_____ **a.** complicated

_____ **b.** new

_____ **c.** basic

2. Distinguishing Fact from Opinion

Two of the statements below present *facts,* which can be proved. The other statement is an *opinion,* which expresses someone's thoughts or beliefs. Label the statements **F** for *fact* and **O** for *opinion.*

_____ **a.** A bike is a compound machine.

_____ **b.** Hammers are more difficult to use than ramps.

_____ **c.** Two or more simple machines can be combined to make a compound machine.

3. Making Correct Inferences

Two of the statements below are correct *inferences,* or reasonable guesses, that are based on information in the article. The other statement is an incorrect, or faulty, inference. Label the statements **C** for *correct* inference and **I** for *incorrect* inference.

_____ **a.** Compound machines have more parts than simple machines.

_____ **b.** The wheels on a car are simple machines.

_____ **c.** A screw would be useful for loading boxes into a truck.

4. Understanding Main Ideas

One of the statements below expresses the main idea of the article. Another statement is too general, or too broad. The other explains only part of the article; it is too narrow. Label the statements **M** for *main idea,* **B** for *too broad,* and **N** for *too narrow.*

_____ **a.** Simple and compound machines make work easier because they enable people to use less force than they would without machines.

_____ **b.** Wheels and axles, levers, and screws are simple machines that help make a bike work.

_____ **c.** Machines are helpful devices that we use every day.

5. Responding to the Article

Complete the following sentence in your own words:

One thing in "Machines: Simple and Compound" that I cannot understand is

_____

_____

D. Expanding Vocabulary

Content-Area Words

Complete each analogy with a word or phrase from the box. Write in the missing word or phrase.

claw	inclined plane	shovel	gears	systems

1. simple machines : alone :: _____ : together

2. spoon : soup :: _____ : dirt

3. lever : hammer :: _____ : ramp

4. lens : camera :: _____ : hammer

5. doors : open :: _____ : turn

Academic English

In the article "Machines: Simple and Compound," you learned that *compound* is an adjective that means "made of more than one part." *Compound* can also be a verb that means "to add to," as in the following sentence.

Throwing garbage into the river will compound the problem of pollution.

Complete the sentence below.

1. Money saved in a bank will *compound* _____

Now use the word *compound* in a sentence of your own.

2. _____

_____

You also learned that *task* means "a job or piece of work." *Task* can describe a job that is easier to do with machines. *Task* can also describe other kinds of jobs, as in the following sentence.

Studying for a test can be a difficult task.

Complete the sentence below.

3. Juan's *task* was to teach the children how to _____

Now use the word *task* in two sentences of your own.

4. _____

5. _____

 Share your new sentences with a partner.

The Spectrum of Light

Before You Read

 Think about what you know. Read the title and the first sentence of the article on the opposite page. What colors do you think make up the light of the Sun?

Vocabulary

The content-area and academic English words below appear in "The Spectrum of Light." Read the definitions and the example sentences.

Content-Area Words

properties (prop′ər tēz) special features of something
Example: We study the *properties* of chemicals to learn how they are different.

wavelength (wāv′lengkth′) the distance between two high points of a wave
Example: A large wave has a longer *wavelength* than a small wave.

spectrum (spek′trəm) the series of colors that white light separates into
Example: A rainbow shows all the colors in the *spectrum* of light.

directions (di rek′shənz) lines that something moves, faces, or lies along
Example: The wind blew the kite in many *directions*.

experiment (iks per′ə mənt) a test used to discover or learn something
Example: A scientist will do an *experiment* to see whether a drug is safe for people.

Academic English

visible (viz′ə bəl) able to be seen
Example: The Moon is not *visible* when the sky is cloudy.

sequence (sē′kwəns) the order things are in
Example: Eight follows seven in the *sequence* of numbers.

Answer the questions below. Circle the part of each question that is the answer. The first one has been done for you.

1. Which has a longer *wavelength*, a ripple in a pond or (a wave in the ocean)?
2. Will you see a group of colors or a group of numbers in the *spectrum?*
3. Which letter comes before *g* in the *sequence* of the alphabet, *f* or *h?*
4. Which is *visible,* air or fog?
5. Are the *properties* of water liquid and clear or solid and blue?
6. Which *directions* are usually at the top and bottom of a map, north and south or east and west?
7. Would you do an *experiment* to learn something or to forget something?

 Now skim the article and look for other words that are new to you. Write each new word and its definition in the Personal Dictionary.

While You Read

Tip! **Think about why you read.** Did you know that we cannot see every type of light? As you read, try to find the names of two types of light that we cannot see.

The Spectrum of Light

1 Although the light of the Sun looks as if it does not have color, it actually does. White light is made up of many colors of light. In the late 17th century, the English scientist Isaac Newton explained how and why white light could be split, or divided, into colors. Now we know that there are different kinds of light. We
5 also know that each kind of light has its own **properties.** This means that each kind of light is different in its own way.

We can see some kinds of light, but not others. Light that we can see is called **visible** light. Light, like other forms of energy, can travel in waves. Different types of light have waves of different lengths. *Wavelength* is a term that scientists use to
10 describe how long or short waves are. Radio waves are a type of invisible light, or light that we cannot see. They have long wavelengths. Visible light and invisible X-rays are types of light that have shorter wavelengths. When different colors of visible light are lined up in order, from longest to shortest in wavelength, they form the **spectrum.**

15 You can see that white light is made up of different colors if you shine it through an angled piece of glass called a prism. All light bends as it passes through glass or water. A straw in a glass of water looks bent because the water bends the light that bounces off the straw. A prism bends light of different wavelengths at different angles, or **directions.** Because the colors of light have
20 different wavelengths, each color bends in a different direction. As white light goes through a prism, the colors bend at different angles and split into the spectrum. Because the wavelength of each color is always the same, the colors of light always split into the same **sequence.** The colors of the spectrum of visible light are red, orange, yellow, green, blue, indigo, and violet. Red light has the
25 longest wavelength, and violet light has the shortest wavelength.

Isaac Newton did an **experiment** to show that a prism does not add or take away anything when light passes through it. He passed white light through a prism to split the light into its spectrum of colors. Then Newton blocked all of the colors of light except the ray of green light. He passed the ray of green light through a
30 second prism. The ray of green light bent as it passed through the prism, but its color did not change. With this experiment, Newton proved that the light of the Sun is made up of many different colors of light.

LANGUAGE CONNECTION

Sometimes the prefix *in-* means "not." In this paragraph, *invisible* means "not visible," or "not able to be seen." Can you think of other words with the prefix *in-?* Hint: What would your homework be if you did not finish it?

CONTENT CONNECTION

A prism splits white light into the spectrum, or a rainbow. We see a rainbow in the sky after it rains because raindrops in the sky act like prisms. What do you think the raindrops do?

After You Read

A. Organizing Ideas

How can you see the spectrum? Complete the sequence chart below. Use the boxes to explain what happens when someone uses a prism to see the spectrum. Write down one event in each box. Refer to the article for help. The first box has been done for you.

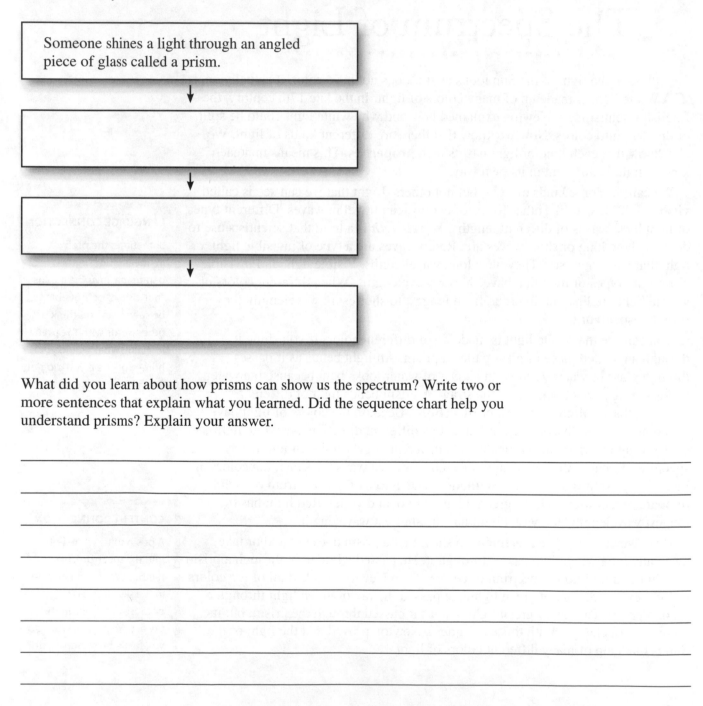

Someone shines a light through an angled piece of glass called a prism.

↓

↓

↓

What did you learn about how prisms can show us the spectrum? Write two or more sentences that explain what you learned. Did the sequence chart help you understand prisms? Explain your answer.

_____

_____

_____

_____

_____

_____

_____

B. Comprehension Skills

Tip! **Think about how to find answers.** Look back at different parts of the text. What facts help you figure out how to complete the sentences?

Mark box **a, b,** or **c** with an **X** before the choice that best completes each sentence.

Recalling Facts

1. A piece of glass that you can use to split light into its different colors is a
   - ☐ **a.** lens.
   - ☐ **b.** mirror.
   - ☐ **c.** prism.

2. Another name for the colors that make up white light is
   - ☐ **a.** an X-ray.
   - ☐ **b.** the spectrum.
   - ☐ **c.** a wavelength.

3. Energy can be measured in
   - ☐ **a.** bandwidths.
   - ☐ **b.** wavelengths.
   - ☐ **c.** stream lengths.

4. In the late 17th century, an experiment showing that white light is made up of other colors was done by
   - ☐ **a.** Aristotle.
   - ☐ **b.** Isaac Newton.
   - ☐ **c.** Albert Einstein.

5. The colors of the spectrum include
   - ☐ **a.** pink, purple, tan, and black.
   - ☐ **b.** brown, silver, white, and gold.
   - ☐ **c.** red, yellow, green, and violet.

Understanding Ideas

1. Although sunlight looks as if it does not have color, it is actually made up of
   - ☐ **a.** pure red light.
   - ☐ **b.** blue and yellow light.
   - ☐ **c.** different colors of light.

2. From the article, you can conclude that orange light is a part of
   - ☐ **a.** white light.
   - ☐ **b.** X-ray light.
   - ☐ **c.** radio waves.

3. The article suggests that X-rays, like other kinds of energy, travel
   - ☐ **a.** in waves.
   - ☐ **b.** as laser beams.
   - ☐ **c.** as low-energy particles.

4. As light passes through water or glass,
   - ☐ **a.** it bends.
   - ☐ **b.** it disappears.
   - ☐ **c.** nothing happens to it.

5. Newton passed green light through a prism to show that there is no change in its
   - ☐ **a.** form.
   - ☐ **b.** color.
   - ☐ **c.** angle.

C. Reading Strategies

1. Recognizing Words in Context

Find the word *bent* in the article. One definition below is closest to the meaning of that word. One definition has the opposite or nearly the opposite meaning. The remaining definition has a meaning that has nothing to do with the other two words. Label the definitions **C** for *closest,* **O** for *opposite* or *nearly opposite,* and **U** for *unrelated.*

_____ **a.** circular

_____ **b.** straight

_____ **c.** crooked

2. Distinguishing Fact from Opinion

Two of the statements below present *facts,* which can be proved. The other statement is an *opinion,* which expresses someone's thoughts or beliefs. Label the statements **F** for *fact* and **O** for *opinion.*

_____ **a.** A prism helps us see the different colors that make up white light.

_____ **b.** Radio waves are a type of invisible light that has long wavelengths.

_____ **c.** The most beautiful color of the spectrum is violet.

3. Making Correct Inferences

Two of the statements below are correct *inferences,* or reasonable guesses, that are based on information in the article. The other statement is an incorrect, or faulty, inference. Label the statements **C** for *correct* inference and **I** for *incorrect* inference.

_____ **a.** The wavelength of each color of light affects where the color fits in the spectrum.

_____ **b.** Even though we cannot always see the different colors in sunlight, they are always there.

_____ **c.** Visible light has very long wavelengths.

4. Understanding Main Ideas

One of the statements below expresses the main idea of the article. Another statement is too general, or too broad. The other explains only part of the article; it is too narrow. Label the statements **M** for *main idea,* **B** for *too broad,* and **N** for *too narrow.*

_____ **a.** When light passes through glass or water, it always bends.

_____ **b.** Today we know about many different types of light, including the white light that comes from the Sun.

_____ **c.** Each type of light has a different wavelength; we can see the spectrum when a prism separates the wavelengths.

5. Responding to the Article

Complete the following sentence in your own words:

Reading "The Spectrum of Light" made me want to learn more about

_____

_____

D. Expanding Vocabulary

Content-Area Words

Complete each sentence with a word from the box. Write the missing word on the line.

wavelength	experiment	properties	spectrum	directions

1. Each kind of light has _____ that make it different from the other kinds.

2. Each color of light has a different _____.

3. The _____ is made up of seven different colors.

4. A prism bends different colors of light in different _____.

5. Isaac Newton did an _____ to show that green light does not change color when it passes through a prism.

Academic English

In the article "The Spectrum of Light," you learned that *visible* means "able to be seen." *Visible* can describe light that can be seen. *Visible* can also describe other things that can be seen, as in the following sentence.

Her happiness was visible on her face after she won a free car.

Complete the sentence below.

1. The sky outside your living room is *visible* if you look out the _____

Now use the word *visible* in a sentence of your own.

2. _____

_____

You also learned that *sequence* means "the order things are in." *Sequence* can describe the order of colors in the spectrum. *Sequence* can also describe the order of other things, as in the following sentence.

Dessert usually comes last in the sequence of a meal.

Complete the sentence below.

3. In the *sequence* of numbers, five comes after _____

Now use the word *sequence* in two sentences of your own.

4. _____

5. _____

 Talk It Over Share your new sentences with a partner.

Recycling Reduces Pollution

Before You Read

Tip! **Think about what you know.** Read the lesson title above. Do you recycle any items at your home or school?

Vocabulary

The content-area and academic English words below appear in "Recycling Reduces Pollution." Read the definitions and the example sentences.

Content-Area Words

pollution (pə lōo′shən) garbage or unhealthy chemicals in the air, water, or soil
    Example: Pollution in our rivers and oceans can hurt fish and other wildlife.

companies (kum′pə nēz) groups of people who work or do business together
    Example: Many companies do business in large cities like New York.

poisonous (poi′zə nəs) full of poison, a substance that may cause sickness or death
    Example: She became sick after she ate a poisonous wild berry.

compost (kom′pōst) a mixture of dead plants and food waste that makes soil healthy
    Example: We use food scraps to make compost that we will spread on our garden soil.

fertilize (furt′əl īz′) to add nutrients, such as minerals, to the soil to help plants grow
    Example: I fertilize the soil in my yard so that the grass gets enough food.

Academic English

dispose (dis pōz′) to get rid (of); to throw away
    Example: People dispose of things they no longer need.

site (sīt) the place where something is
    Example: Washington, D.C., is the site of the U.S. Capitol building.

Read again the example sentences that follow the content-area and academic English word definitions. With a partner, discuss the meanings of the words and sentences. Then make up a sentence of your own for each word. Your teacher may wish to discuss your new sentences in class.

 Now skim the article and look for other words that are new to you. Write each new word and its definition in the Personal Dictionary.

While You Read

Tip! **Think about why you read.** People who recycle help keep the environment clean. Do you think recycling is important? As you read, think about the ways recycling can help the environment.

Recycling Reduces Pollution

1   Most families in the United States throw away almost 3,000 kilograms (about 3 tons) of trash each year. Paper, plastics, glass, and cans make up more than half of the trash we throw away. Food waste, or garbage from food, makes up another large portion of our trash. People in the United States use millions of glass
5   bottles and metal cans every day. Much of this glass and metal simply becomes garbage, but some people recycle their bottles and cans. Other people can use these recycled bottles and cans to make new things.

Pollution from waste is a very big problem. Waste disposal **companies** are companies that help **dispose** of, or get rid of, garbage. They take away
10   garbage and bury it in landfills. Landfills are places where people bury garbage underground. Many landfills are full, and it can be hard to find a **site** for a new landfill in some areas. Over time, trash slowly dissolves, or melts, into chemicals. Some of these chemicals are **poisonous** and can pollute water. Another way to dispose of trash is to burn it. At incineration plants, people burn trash to make
15   energy. Although this is a good way to make use of trash, some of the gas made through the process pollutes the air.

To reduce, or cut down on, the pollution made by waste, people can try to make less trash. They can do this by "reducing, reusing, and recycling" trash.

To reduce trash, people use fewer new things. One way to use fewer new things
20   is to write on both sides of a sheet of paper. Another way is to carry cloth bags when you shop. A third way is to buy things made from recycled materials.

To reuse something, people can save bags, containers such as boxes or jars, clothing, books, and toys. People can wash and reuse plastic bags and containers. They can use clothing, books, and toys again or give them to other people.

25   To recycle something, people can separate things that can be used again to make new products. Paper, cans, glass, and plastic can be recycled. In many cities and towns, workers pick up recyclables (things that can be recycled) from people's homes. People who live in towns that do not have pickup workers may need to bring their recyclables to a recycling center near their home.

30   Another way to recycle is to use food waste to make **compost.** People can pile food waste (such as vegetable and fruit scraps, tea leaves, and coffee grounds) outside in a wooden box. Straw and dead leaves can also go into the box. The food waste, straw, and leaves break down and become compost. People can use the compost to **fertilize** gardens. If we reduce, reuse, and recycle the products we use
35   every day, we can cut down on trash and pollution.

CONTENT CONNECTION

Who picks up your garbage? Many cities and towns use tax money to pay workers to pick up garbage. What problems might occur if no one picked up garbage?

LANGUAGE CONNECTION

Sometimes the prefix *re-* means "again." If you *reuse* something, you use it again. Can you think of other words that begin with *re-* and mean "to do (something) again"? Hint: Think of the word you use when you read something again.

After You Read

A. Organizing Ideas

How can we reduce pollution? Complete the outline below. Write down two or more examples of ways people can reduce pollution by reducing, reusing, or recycling. Refer to the article to help you. Some have been done for you.

A. Reduce Trash

  1. Buy things made from recycled material such as paper, glass, or plastic.

  2. _____

  _____

  3. _____

  _____

B. _____

  1. Use plastic bags and containers more than once.

  _____

  2. _____

  _____

  3. _____

  _____

C. Recycle Something

  1. Recycle cans, glass items, and paper.

  _____

  2. _____

  _____

  3. _____

  _____

How did completing the outline help you? What did you learn about reducing pollution? Write two or more sentences about ways you could reduce, reuse, or recycle.

_____

_____

B. Comprehension Skills

Tip! **Think about how to find answers.** Look back at what you read. The information is in the text, but you may have to look in several sentences to find it.

Mark box **a, b,** or **c** with an **X** before the choice that best completes each sentence.

Recalling Facts

1. Each year, most families in the United States throw away about
   ☐ **a.** half a ton of trash.
   ☐ **b.** 3 tons of trash.
   ☐ **c.** 5 tons of trash.

2. Waste disposal companies take trash away and bury it in areas called
   ☐ **a.** landfills.
   ☐ **b.** volcanoes.
   ☐ **c.** wells.

3. Making new things out of old things is
   ☐ **a.** disposal.
   ☐ **b.** pollution.
   ☐ **c.** recycling.

4. At incineration plants, people
   ☐ **a.** bury trash.
   ☐ **b.** burn trash.
   ☐ **c.** melt trash into chemicals.

5. One way to cut down on pollution caused by waste is to
   ☐ **a.** reuse more goods.
   ☐ **b.** build more landfills.
   ☐ **c.** burn chemical waste.

Understanding Ideas

1. Garbage disposal is a problem in the United States because
   ☐ **a.** pollution is destroying many cities.
   ☐ **b.** there are fewer and fewer places to bury garbage.
   ☐ **c.** there are not enough recycling centers to handle the material.

2. Recycling decreases pollution by
   ☐ **a.** reducing trash.
   ☐ **b.** making more trash.
   ☐ **c.** burning trash.

3. Old landfills may
   ☐ **a.** take up space that should be used for glass factories.
   ☐ **b.** cause more pollution than cars do.
   ☐ **c.** contain poisonous chemicals that can leak into underground water.

4. Someone who finds stale food in a refrigerator could reduce waste by
   ☐ **a.** throwing it in the garbage.
   ☐ **b.** putting it in a compost pile.
   ☐ **c.** taking it to a recycling center.

5. From the article, you can conclude that the amount of household waste that is thrown away is
   ☐ **a.** too much.
   ☐ **b.** just right.
   ☐ **c.** not enough.

C. Reading Strategies

1. Recognizing Words in Context

Find the word *save* in the article. One definition below is closest to the meaning of that word. One definition has the opposite or nearly the opposite meaning. The remaining definition has a meaning that has nothing to do with the other two words. Label the definitions **C** for *closest*, **O** for *opposite* or *nearly opposite*, and **U** for *unrelated*.

_____ **a.** waste

_____ **b.** keep

_____ **c.** like

2. Distinguishing Fact from Opinion

Two of the statements below present *facts*, which can be proved. The other statement is an *opinion*, which expresses someone's thoughts or beliefs. Label the statements **F** for *fact* and **O** for *opinion*.

_____ **a.** In the United States, millions of bottles and cans are used every day.

_____ **b.** The easiest way to fertilize plants is to use compost.

_____ **c.** Trash that people burn at incineration plants can pollute the air.

3. Making Correct Inferences

Two of the statements below are correct *inferences,* or reasonable guesses, that are based on information in the article. The other statement is an incorrect, or faulty, inference. Label the statements **C** for *correct* inference and **I** for *incorrect* inference.

_____ **a.** One way to reduce the amount of new paper people use is to buy recycled paper.

_____ **b.** One way to recycle is to take trash to a landfill.

_____ **c.** One way to reuse an item is to keep money in an old jar.

4. Understanding Main Ideas

One of the statements below expresses the main idea of the article. Another statement is too general, or too broad. The other explains only part of the article; it is too narrow. Label the statements **M** for *main idea,* **B** for *too broad,* and **N** for *too narrow.*

_____ **a.** Not all towns have workers to pick up recyclables.

_____ **b.** To reduce air and water pollution, we must recycle, reduce, and reuse trash.

_____ **c.** It is important for everyone to recycle at home and at school.

5. Responding to the Article

Complete the following sentence in your own words:

By reading "Recycling Reduces Pollution," I learned

_____

_____

D. Expanding Vocabulary

Content-Area Words

Cross out one word or phrase in each row that is not related to the word in dark type.

1. **pollution**   gas   air   child   water
2. **companies**   animals   together   work   people
3. **poisonous**   safe   dangerous   dirty   chemicals
4. **compost**   food waste   dead plants   clothing   fertilizer
5. **fertilize**   gardens   healthy   plants   streets

Academic English

In the article "Recycling Reduces Pollution," you learned that *dispose* means "to get rid (of)" or "to throw away." *Dispose* can also mean "to make someone or something likely to be affected by something," as in the following sentence.

    The child's habit of eating sugary cereals will dispose his teeth to cavities.

Complete the sentence below.

1. Keisha's shyness does not *dispose* her to enjoy speaking to_____

Now use the word *dispose* in a sentence of your own.

2. _____

_____

You also learned that *site* means "the place where something is." *Site* can refer to the place where a landfill is. *Site* can also refer to places where other things are, as in the following sentence.

    The site of my vacation will be Jalisco, Mexico.

Complete the sentence below.

3. A forest is a *site* where many trees _____

Now use the word *site* in two sentences of your own.

4. _____

5. _____

Share your new sentences with a partner.

Writing a Brochure

Read the brochure. Then complete the sentences. Use words from the Word Bank.

Visit Beautiful Sandy Beach

Don't wait!

Schedule your visit now!

Can you imagine yourself walking along the (1) _____ and enjoying salty air and a light breeze? Then you belong at Sandy Beach! Walk along the coast when the (2) _____ rise and fall. Swim in the cool, beautiful water—so clear that the sandy bottom is (3) _____ for miles out into the ocean! There is natural beauty in all (4) _____, no matter where you look. Some visitors say that they feel (5) _____ happiness when they see Sandy Beach. Join us soon for a relaxing ocean vacation!

Word Bank

tides	directions
instant	seashore
visible	

Reading a Newspaper

Read the newspaper article. Circle the word that completes each sentence.

Daily News • Science

Area Businesses Need to Clean Up
by Man Kai Chan

City leaders have just discovered that several large (**experiments, companies**) doing business in our area dumped dangerous chemicals into a local river last month. Citizens are worried about the pollution in their water. They think that (**exposed, eventually**) the pollution may cause health problems. The businesses have promised to clean up the mess, even though it will be a (**challenge, spectrum**). They also have agreed to (**record, dispose**) of all waste safely in the future. City leaders say that unless we keep a close watch on how local businesses care for the environment, we will (**compound, fertilize**) our pollution problems.

 **Making Connections**

Work with a partner. Talk about what the words mean. How can you use the words to talk about building a house? List your ideas in the outline of the house below.

enclosed	error	reversed	claw	inclined plane
shovel	systems	task	sequence	site

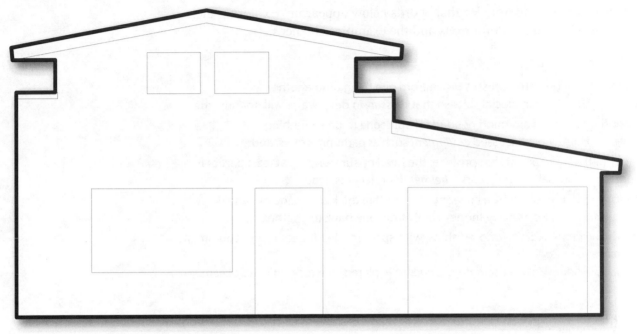

Use all of the words above in a paragraph of your own. Each sentence may include one or more of the words. To help you start writing, look at the ideas you wrote about. After you write your sentences, read them over. If you find a mistake, correct it.

_____

_____

_____

_____

_____

_____

_____

_____

_____

Before You Read

 Think about what you know. Read the title and the first two sentences of the article on the opposite page. What do you think the article may be about? Have you ever explored the world under the sea?

Vocabulary

The content-area and academic English words below appear in "Exploring the Undersea World." Read the definitions and the example sentences.

Content-Area Words

pressure (presh′ər) force that presses down from one thing onto another
Example: Divers wear special suits so that *pressure* in deep water will not hurt them.

equipment (i kwip′mənt) anything needed for someone to do something
Example: Hockey players need *equipment* such as padding, skates, and sticks.

helmet (hel′mit) a cover or hat that protects the head by surrounding at least part of it
Example: A football player wears a *helmet* to protect his head.

armored (är′mərd) protected by a covering that is often thick and made of metal
Example: *Armored* cars carry money safely from one bank to another.

bathyscaphes (bath′i skāfs′) armored ships, with space inside for people and equipment, that explore deep underwater
Example: Scientists may use *bathyscaphes* to explore shipwrecks in deep oceans.

Academic English

linked (lingkt) connected
Example: Her keys are *linked* to a key chain.

vehicles (vē′ə kəlz) machines that move people or things from one place to another
Example: People drive *vehicles* such as buses, cars, and trucks.

Complete the sentences below that contain the content-area and academic English words above. Use the spaces provided. The first one has been done for you.

1. Your television set will not work if it is not *linked* to a source of ___electricity___.

2. You should wear a *helmet* when you ride your bike to _____.

3. *Bathyscaphes* allow people to explore places that are _____.

4. You can put *pressure* on a cut to _____.

5. *Vehicles* need new tires when _____.

6. In order to cook food, you might use *equipment* such as _____.

7. Soldiers in wars once wore *armored* suits to _____.

 Now skim the article and look for other words that are new to you. Write each new word and its definition in the Personal Dictionary.

While You Read

Tip! **Think about why you read.** Have you ever thought about diving deep underwater to explore? How would you breathe? Read the article to find the answer.

Exploring the Undersea World

1 Early in history, people could not explore most parts of the world that are deep underwater for two reasons: they could not breathe underwater, and they could not survive the huge amount of **pressure** deep in the sea. The average "free" diver, or person trained to swim deep underwater without equipment, cannot stay
5 underwater for more than three minutes without coming up for air. The best divers can hold their breath, or go without breathing, for even longer—and can dive to more than 10 meters (33 feet) below the surface, or top, of the water.

To learn more about the ocean world, people needed to find a way to breathe underwater. Pictures and writings from thousands of years ago show that long,
10 hollow tubes and pipes enabled divers to breathe air from the surface. However, they could not dive very deep.

Hundreds of years ago, people started to build diving **equipment** to try to solve these problems. In the 17th century, divers tried to use a tight **helmet** with a long breathing tube made of leather, or dried animal skins. The tube was **linked** to a
15 closed container of air above the surface of the water. The problem was that there was no way for fresh air to get into the container. Used air filled the helmet, and the diver could not breathe. Some inventors built diving bells, which were upside-down metal containers that held air underwater. Divers could go into the diving bell to breathe, but after a while the fresh air got used up in these too.

20 In the late 1830s in London, Augustus Siebe built a diving suit. It had a metal helmet and a metal cover that went over the top part of the diver's body. Air pumped from the surface went through a hollow pipe into the helmet. This suit let a diver go deep because it kept the body safe from the pressure of water. In the mid-20th century, Jacques Cousteau and Emile Gagnan invented diving equipment called
25 scuba gear. Scuba gear allowed divers to carry tanks, or containers, of air on their backs. It let divers spend more time underwater and move through the water more easily. Today new **armored** suits let divers go to depths of 760 meters (2,500 feet).

New inventions helped people build underwater chambers (rooms or spaces) and **vehicles.** Chambers that keep water out and air in could be lowered from
30 boats to depths of 1 kilometer (3,200 feet). Vehicles called **bathyscaphes** helped people learn about the deep sea. In 1960 Jacques Picard piloted, or drove, a bathyscaphe called *Trieste* to what was known as the deepest part of the ocean.

Today remote-controlled vehicles, or vehicles that are controlled by people outside of them, are used to explore the deep ocean. These machines can record
35 information and bring back things to help us learn more about the undersea world as well as our planet.

CONTENT CONNECTION

Water puts pressure on a diver's lungs, the organ that permits a person to breathe. The pressure increases as the diver goes deeper. At a depth of 33 feet, the lungs are under twice as much pressure as they are at sea level. What do you think this might feel like?

LANGUAGE CONNECTION

Remote means "far away." A remote-controlled television lets viewers change channels from a distance.

After You Read

A. Organizing Ideas

How has diving equipment changed throughout history? Complete the time line below. In each box, write one example of a type of diving equipment. If the article mentions a time in history when the equipment was used, write that information on the line above the box. The first box has been done for you.

Types of Diving Equipment

thousands of years ago

> "free" diving; long, hollow tubes that reached above the surface

How has diving equipment improved throughout history? Write two or more sentences to answer this question. Did the time line help you answer this question? Why or why not?

_____

_____

_____

B. Comprehension Skills

 Think about how to find answers. Think about what each sentence means. Try to say it to yourself in your own words before you complete it.

Mark box **a, b,** or **c** with an **X** before the choice that best completes each sentence.

Recalling Facts

1. Tubes and pipes above the surface let early divers
   - ☐ **a.** breathe underwater.
   - ☐ **b.** swim faster than ever before.
   - ☐ **c.** protect themselves from water pressure.

2. The first diving suits did not let divers
   - ☐ **a.** rise to the surface.
   - ☐ **b.** talk to each other underwater.
   - ☐ **c.** breathe fresh air for very long.

3. The first diving suits that protected the body from water pressure were made of
   - ☐ **a.** cloth.
   - ☐ **b.** metal.
   - ☐ **c.** leather.

4. The deepest known part of the ocean
   - ☐ **a.** has never been reached by humans.
   - ☐ **b.** has been reached by a diver in scuba gear.
   - ☐ **c.** has been reached by humans in undersea vehicles.

5. An invention by Jacques Cousteau and Emile Gagnan helps divers carry
   - ☐ **a.** helmets.
   - ☐ **b.** air tanks.
   - ☐ **c.** diving bells.

Understanding Ideas

1. A device that allows divers to breathe underwater for a long period of time is
   - ☐ **a.** an air tank.
   - ☐ **b.** metal armor.
   - ☐ **c.** a remote-controlled vehicle.

2. A device that protects the body from water pressure is
   - ☐ **a.** a diving bell.
   - ☐ **b.** an armored diving suit.
   - ☐ **c.** a leather breathing tube.

3. A bathyscaphe is
   - ☐ **a.** an underwater vehicle.
   - ☐ **b.** a special kind of bathtub.
   - ☐ **c.** a means of escaping when divers run out of air.

4. From the article, you can conclude that pieces of rock from the ocean floor are helpful to scientists because they
   - ☐ **a.** are valuable minerals.
   - ☐ **b.** are meteorites from outer space.
   - ☐ **c.** may tell them about the history of Earth.

5. You can also conclude that diving gear has
   - ☐ **a.** allowed people to explore the ocean.
   - ☐ **b.** had no effect on the study of the ocean.
   - ☐ **c.** prevented people from exploring the ocean.

C. Reading Strategies

1. Recognizing Words in Context

Find the word *hollow* in the article. One definition below is closest to the meaning of that word. One definition has the opposite or nearly the opposite meaning. The remaining definition has a meaning that has nothing to do with the other two words. Label the definitions **C** for *closest,* **O** for *opposite* or *nearly opposite,* and **U** for *unrelated.*

_____ **a.** shiny and bright

_____ **b.** empty

_____ **c.** solid or filled

2. Distinguishing Fact from Opinion

Two of the statements below present *facts,* which can be proved. The other statement is an *opinion,* which expresses someone's thoughts or beliefs. Label the statements **F** for *fact* and **O** for *opinion.*

_____ **a.** At one time, a diver who was not wearing armor might have been hurt underwater.

_____ **b.** A bathyscaphe is a type of boat.

_____ **c.** Divers must have been scared to use diving bells.

3. Making Correct Inferences

Two of the statements below are correct *inferences,* or reasonable guesses, that are based on information in the article. The other statement is an incorrect, or faulty, inference. Label the statements **C** for *correct* inference and **I** for *incorrect* inference.

_____ **a.** The equipment used for diving has changed in many ways.

_____ **b.** Once diving bells ran out of oxygen, they were no longer useful to divers.

_____ **c.** Bathyscaphes are driven only by remote control.

4. Understanding Main Ideas

One of the statements below expresses the main idea of the article. Another statement is too general, or too broad. The other explains only part of the article; it is too narrow. Label the statements **M** for *main idea,* **B** for *too broad,* and **N** for *too narrow.*

_____ **a.** Divers have tried many inventions to keep themselves safe.

_____ **b.** Jacques Picard explored the deepest known part of the ocean.

_____ **c.** A diver needs many kinds of equipment to explore the ocean safely.

5. Responding to the Article

Complete the following sentence in your own words:

What interested me most in "Exploring the Undersea World" was

_____

_____

D. Expanding Vocabulary

Content-Area Words

Read each item carefully. Write on the line the word or phrase that best completes each sentence.

1. Divers wear _____ to protect their bodies from water pressure.
   helmets   armor   tubes

2. Special equipment helps divers carry _____ for breathing underwater.
   air tanks   air hoses   armored suits

3. Tight helmets with long _____ were worn by divers years ago.
   diving bells   chambers   breathing tubes

4. The armored suits divers wear today allow them to go _____ meters underwater.
   760   200   1,400

5. There is room for people and _____ in bathyscaphes.
   tubes   vehicles   equipment

Academic English

In the article "Exploring the Undersea World," you learned that *linked* means "connected." *Linked* can describe how early diving helmets were connected to containers of air. *Linked* can also describe how other things are connected, as in the following sentence.

Your arms are linked to your body at the shoulders.

Complete the sentence below.

1. Because of his previous arrests, the suspect was *linked* to_____

Now use the word *linked* in a sentence of your own.

2. _____

You also learned that *vehicles* are "machines that move people or things from one place to another." *Vehicles* can also be "means through which things can be expressed or displayed," as in the following sentence.

Plays and poetry are vehicles for expressing ideas.

Complete the sentence below.

3. Movies are *vehicles* for _____

Now use the word *vehicles* in two sentences of your own.

4. _____

5. _____

 Share your new sentences with a partner.

The Endangered Everglades

Before You Read

 Think about what you know. Read the lesson title above. What do you predict the article will be about? Do you know of any animals or plants that are endangered?

Vocabulary

The content-area and academic English words below appear in "The Endangered Everglades." Read the definitions and the example sentences.

Content-Area Words

endangered (en dān′jərd) in danger of dying out or disappearing
  Example: Zoos protect *endangered* animals by giving them safe environments.

environmental (en vī′rən ment′əl) relating to the world around a plant or an animal
  Example: People cause many *environmental* changes that affect animals.

concentrated (kon′sən trāt′əd) grouped in one place
  Example: Large numbers of people are often *concentrated* in cities.

predators (pred′ə tərz) animals that hunt and eat other animals
  Example: Lions are dangerous *predators* of many animals in Africa.

disturbs (dis turbz′) bothers; changes the way something normally is
  Example: Too much noise *disturbs* my sleep.

Academic English

ensure (en shoor′) to make sure
  Example: You should study to *ensure* your success on the test.

strategy (strat′ə jē) a plan for how to get something done
  Example: The soccer coach had a *strategy* to help his team win.

Rate each vocabulary word according to the following scale. Write a number next to each content-area and academic English word.

4   I have never seen the word before.

3   I have seen the word but do not know what it means.

2   I know what the word means when I read it.

1   I use the word myself in speaking or writing.

 Now skim the article and look for other words that are new to you. Write each new word and its definition in the Personal Dictionary.

While You Read

 Think about why you read. Do you do things, such as recycling, to help protect the environment? As you read, look for one way people have harmed the Everglades and one way people can help protect them.

The Endangered Everglades

1　Everglades National Park in Florida is a home for many living things. A grassy river of slow-moving water makes life possible for the plants and animals of this region. Water flows more than 160 kilometers (100 miles) from Lake Okeechobee to wet, grassy areas called marshes at the edge of the sea. Many
5　trees, plants, and animals live in forests on islands in the river. Other trees, such as cypress and mangrove, grow right in the water. Some birds walk through the water between the trees, eating the shrimp and fish that swim there.

　　Many **endangered** plants and animals live within Everglades National Park. One of the endangered plants is Garber's spurge. This plant is one of more than
10　1,000 kinds of plants that grow in the park. The American crocodile, a bird called the wood stork, and a large cat called the Florida panther are just a few of the endangered animals that live in the park. The plants and animals in the Everglades are not all that is in danger of dying out. The Everglades area itself is in danger. Because the Everglades area is a national park, the U.S. government tries to
15　protect it. However, this protection has not been enough to **ensure** that it is safe from **environmental** changes.

　　The Everglades area has changed in many ways because of the way people in Florida have used water. Some developers (people who develop land or build things on it) have drained water out of wetlands to build new homes and roads.
20　Homes and farms now use some of the water that once flowed through the Everglades. Because less water is flowing through the park, endangered birds, such as the wood stork and the snail kite, have less food.

　　The Everglades has a dry season that is an important feeding time for some animals. As the river dries up into small pools of water, fish and other food
25　sources become **concentrated** in small areas. This makes them easy for **predators** to catch and eat. But sometimes rainstorms occur during this season. When it rains, cities and neighborhoods move the extra water into the Everglades to stop their streets from flooding. This fills up the river again and **disturbs** the food supply for Everglades predators. It also washes away bird, crocodile, and alligator
30　eggs. Some of these animals are endangered.

　　To save plant and animal life and the Everglades park itself, the government has added new land to the park. The land gives animals more room to find food and to build homes such as nests, but it does not solve the water problem. To solve the water problem, people will have to work together to protect the Everglades. They
35　will need to find a **strategy** to control the water in Florida.

CONTENT CONNECTION

The United States has 388 national parks, including endangered lands, historic sites, and national monuments. Have you ever visited a national park?

LANGUAGE CONNECTION

Rainstorm is a compound noun made of two other nouns: *rain* and *storm*. Can you find the compound noun in the previous paragraph? What do you think it means?

After You Read

A. Organizing Ideas

What are some important facts about the Everglades? Complete the boxes below. For each paragraph, write the main idea on the top line. Then write down one detail that supports each main idea. Refer to the article for help. Some have been done for you.

Paragraph 1

Main Idea: The Everglades is a wet, grassy area in Florida that has many plants and animals.

• Many trees, plants, and animals live on islands in the river.

Paragraph 2

Main Idea: The Everglades and many of its plants and animals are endangered.

• _____

Paragraph 3

Main Idea: _____

• Developers have drained water to build homes and roads, so there is less food for many endangered birds.

Paragraph 4

Main Idea: _____

• _____

Paragraph 5

Main Idea: _____

• _____

What are the most important facts about the Everglades? Write two or more sentences that would explain the Everglades and its problems to someone. How did this activity help you decide what to say?

_____

_____

_____

B. Comprehension Skills

Tip! **Think about how to find answers.** Read each sentence below. Underline the words that will help you figure out how to complete each item.

Mark box **a, b,** or **c** with an **X** before the choice that best completes each sentence.

Recalling Facts

1. To stay alive, the plants and animals in the Everglades need the
   - ☐ **a.** glacier.
   - ☐ **b.** grassy river.
   - ☐ **c.** large pine forest.

2. The American crocodile, the wood stork, and the Florida panther are
   - ☐ **a.** endangered animals of the Everglades.
   - ☐ **b.** living in large groups in the Everglades.
   - ☐ **c.** creatures that no longer live in the Everglades.

3. Garber's spurge is a type of
   - ☐ **a.** fish.
   - ☐ **b.** plant.
   - ☐ **c.** insect.

4. The new land that the U.S. government added to the park has
   - ☐ **a.** solved all the problems in the Everglades.
   - ☐ **b.** solved the water problem in the Everglades.
   - ☐ **c.** given animals more room to find food and build homes.

5. Nature in the Everglades has changed in many ways because of
   - ☐ **a.** a lack of rain.
   - ☐ **b.** very cold temperatures.
   - ☐ **c.** the way people use water in the area.

Understanding Ideas

1. Without water, life in the Everglades
   - ☐ **a.** would not survive.
   - ☐ **b.** would change in order to survive.
   - ☐ **c.** would not change.

2. When people move extra water to the park in the dry season, the water
   - ☐ **a.** helps the animals.
   - ☐ **b.** harms the animals.
   - ☐ **c.** does not affect the animals.

3. To solve the water problem in the Everglades, people need to
   - ☐ **a.** stop using water.
   - ☐ **b.** close the national park.
   - ☐ **c.** find ways to protect nature while meeting human needs for water.

4. A visitor to Everglades National Park will probably see
   - ☐ **a.** cactus plants.
   - ☐ **b.** trees growing in water.
   - ☐ **c.** a snow-covered mountain peak.

5. Lands that are protected by the government can be
   - ☐ **a.** kept safe from any harm.
   - ☐ **b.** harmful to places around them.
   - ☐ **c.** harmed by what takes place outside them.

C. Reading Strategies

1. Recognizing Words in Context

Find the word *flows* in the article. One definition below is closest to the meaning of that word. One definition has the opposite or nearly the opposite meaning. The remaining definition has a meaning that has nothing to do with the other two words. Label the definitions **C** for *closest,* **O** for *opposite* or *nearly opposite,* and **U** for *unrelated.*

_____ **a.** whispers

_____ **b.** stops

_____ **c.** moves

2. Distinguishing Fact from Opinion

Two of the statements below present *facts,* which can be proved. The other statement is an *opinion,* which expresses someone's thoughts or beliefs. Label the statements **F** for *fact* and **O** for *opinion.*

_____ **a.** The American crocodile is an endangered animal.

_____ **b.** The government should try harder to protect the Everglades.

_____ **c.** Many animals find food in the water of the Everglades.

3. Making Correct Inferences

Two of the statements below are correct *inferences,* or reasonable guesses, that are based on information in the article. The other statement is an incorrect, or faulty, inference. Label the statements **C** for *correct* inference and **I** for *incorrect* inference.

_____ **a.** Things people do have affected life in the Everglades.

_____ **b.** The dry season helps keep the right numbers of prey and predators in the Everglades.

_____ **c.** Many types of animals have left the Everglades because it is dangerous.

4. Understanding Main Ideas

One of the statements below expresses the main idea of the article. Another statement is too general, or too broad. The other explains only part of the article; it is too narrow. Label the statements **M** for *main idea,* **B** for *too broad,* and **N** for *too narrow.*

_____ **a.** Farmers are using some of the water that once flowed through the Everglades.

_____ **b.** To protect the endangered plants and animals of the Everglades, we must learn how to control Florida's water supply.

_____ **c.** Many endangered plants and animals live in Everglades National Park in Florida.

5. Responding to the Article

Complete the following sentence in your own words:

Before reading "The Endangered Everglades," I already knew

_____

_____

D. Expanding Vocabulary

Content-Area Words

Complete each sentence with a word from the box. Write the missing word on the line.

endangered	environmental	concentrated	predators	disturbs

1. Water from cities _____ the food supply in the Everglades.

2. Many shrimp and fish were _____ in the small pool of water.

3. The Florida panther and the snail kite are both _____.

4. Many _____ eat fish from the river that flows through the Everglades.

5. We need to protect national parks from _____ changes.

Academic English

In the article "The Endangered Everglades," you learned that *ensure* means "to make sure." *Ensure* can describe how people try to make sure that the Everglades area is protected. *Ensure* can also describe how people or things make sure of other things, as in the following sentence.

Plenty of rain and sunshine will ensure that your plants grow.

Complete the sentence below.

1. Many animals have thick fur to *ensure* that they stay_____

Now use the word *ensure* in a sentence of your own.

2. _____

_____

You also learned that *strategy* means "a plan for how to get something done." *Strategy* can describe a plan to protect the Everglades. *Strategy* can also describe other plans to get something done, as in the following sentence.

Her strategy helped her win the game of chess.

Complete the sentence below.

3. Studying is a good *strategy* to help you do well on a _____

Now use the word *strategy* in two sentences of your own.

4. _____

5. _____

 Share your new sentences with a partner.

Before You Read

 Think about what you know. Read the title and first two sentences of the article on the opposite page. Have you ever seen a movie or read a story about someone who survived in the forest alone? What did the person eat?

Vocabulary

The content-area and academic English words below appear in "A Meal of Wild Forest Plants." Read the definitions and the example sentences.

Content-Area Words

clover (klō′vər) plants that have small green leaves that have three or four parts
Example: In one part of the forest, the ground is covered with green *clover.*

tubers (tōō′bərz) large, fleshy parts of underground roots that store food for a plant
Example: Potatoes are *tubers* that are delicious to eat.

acorns (ā′kôrnz) nuts that grow on oak trees and are partly covered by a woody cup
Example: Squirrels store *acorns* to eat in the winter.

bitter (bit′ər) having a sharp, unpleasant taste
Example: Fruit that is not ripe often has a *bitter* taste.

thorns (thôrnz) short, sharp points on the stem or branches of a plant
Example: Rosebushes have beautiful flowers but sharp *thorns.*

Academic English

extract (iks trakt′) to take something out of something else
Example: It can be difficult to *extract* one chemical from a mixture.

expert (eks′purt) someone who knows a great deal about a subject
Example: A doctor is an *expert* on health and the body.

Answer the questions below. Circle the part of each question that is the answer. The first one has been done for you.

1. Do *acorns* grow (on a tree) or under the ground?
2. Is *clover* a fruit with seeds or a plant with leaves?
3. If you wanted to talk to an *expert* on animals, would you call a musician or a veterinarian?
4. If you wanted to taste something *bitter,* would you try a green banana or a piece of cake?
5. If doctors need to *extract* something from inside the body, would they perform surgery or take an X-ray?
6. Would you find *tubers* under the ground or inside a fruit?
7. Would *thorns* make a plant sweet to eat or dangerous to touch?

 Now skim the article and look for other words that are new to you. Write each new word and its definition in the Personal Dictionary.

While You Read

 Think about why you read. Have you ever eaten wild forest plants? Do you know which plants are safe to eat? As you read, look for four kinds of plants that are safe for people to eat.

A Meal of Wild Forest Plants

1 Many wild plants in the United States are edible, which means that we can eat them. The part of the plant that we can eat depends on the type of plant. Some plants have underground roots that are edible. Other edible plant parts may include the stems, leaves, seeds, or even flowers. Edible plants grow at different
5 times of the year and in different places. You could make a whole meal of forest plants. In autumn this meal might include watercress salad, arrowhead soup, acorn bread, and gooseberry pie. You would need to find watercress leaves, arrowhead roots, acorns, and gooseberries to make this meal.

Watercress grows in wet places, such as springs (places where water comes out
10 of the ground) or the edges of rivers. To find this plant, a person would look for large areas of leaves that look like **clover** and are attached to tall reddish stalks, or stems. These stalks should be growing sideways in water. Watercress roots are white, and the small, four-petal flowers can be white or yellow. You can eat watercress raw, or without cooking it, in a salad or cooked with steam, like spinach.

15 A person looking for arrowhead roots would probably wear old clothes, because this is a dirty job. The arrowhead plant grows in mud near ponds and rivers. To find this plant, a person would look for a plant with arrow-shaped leaves and flowers that have three round white petals. The flowers grow on a single stem. In the fall, arrowhead roots grow potatolike **tubers** that taste good with wild
20 onions in soups. Arrowhead tubers grow about 30 centimeters (12 inches) below the ground and about 1 meter (3¼ feet) from the stalk of the plant. You can use gardening tools, such as rakes or shovels, to find them in the mud.

In early autumn, **acorns** fall from oak trees. A substance called tannin makes the acorns taste **bitter.** After you take the shells off the acorns, you need to soak
25 them in water for a few days or cook them in boiling water a few times to **extract** the tannin. When the acorns are not bitter anymore, you can bake them in an oven and grind, or smash, them to make flour for bread.

Gooseberries grow in open areas of the forest. Gooseberries are small and round. They can be white, red, yellow, or green. They grow on small bushes, or
30 shrubs, and they become ripe and ready to eat in autumn. To be sure that a shrub is really a gooseberry shrub, look for **thorns.** Also, look for hand-shaped leaves that look like they have three or five fingers. You can bake the berries of the gooseberry shrub in a pie.

Only a person who is an **expert** on wild plants should find them for meals. Some
35 poisonous wild plants look like edible plants, but poisonous plants can make you very sick if you eat them. Sometimes poisonous plants can even cause death.

LANGUAGE CONNECTION

Autumn is one of the four seasons. *Autumn* is a synonym for *fall,* which means that the two words have about the same meaning. Can you name the other three seasons?

CONTENT CONNECTION

Have you ever picked up an acorn in the fall? Some animals, such as squirrels, pick up fallen acorns and save them to eat during the winter. Have you ever seen a squirrel carrying an acorn in its mouth?

After You Read

A. Organizing Ideas

What forest plants are edible? Complete the chart below. Fill in the missing information about the four edible plants you read about. Use the article to help you. Some have been done for you.

Edible Plant	Description	Location	How to Eat It
watercress			
			in arrowhead soup
		grow on oak trees	
	small berries on shrubs; berries can be white, red, yellow, or green; shrubs have hand-shaped leaves with 3 or 5 "fingers"		

Could you make a meal of wild forest plants? Choose one of the plants in the chart. Write two or more sentences about what you would do to find the plant and make food from it. Did the chart help you decide what you would do? Why or why not?

_____

_____

_____

_____

B. Comprehension Skills

Tip! **Think about how to find answers.** Read each sentence below. Underline the words that will help you figure out how to complete each item.

Mark box **a, b,** or **c** with an **X** before the choice that best completes each sentence.

Recalling Facts

1. Edible plants are plants that
   - ☐ **a.** we can eat.
   - ☐ **b.** we cannot eat.
   - ☐ **c.** are poisonous.

2. An edible plant that grows in springs or along rivers is
   - ☐ **a.** a cactus.
   - ☐ **b.** an apple.
   - ☐ **c.** watercress.

3. An edible potatolike tuber that grows in the mud is
   - ☐ **a.** a pumpkin.
   - ☐ **b.** a gooseberry.
   - ☐ **c.** an arrowhead root.

4. Oak trees produce
   - ☐ **a.** acorns.
   - ☐ **b.** pine nuts.
   - ☐ **c.** arrowhead roots.

5. Small round gooseberries grow
   - ☐ **a.** on shrubs with thorns.
   - ☐ **b.** on large trees with no thorns.
   - ☐ **c.** on underwater stalks with no leaves.

Understanding Ideas

1. A tuber is a
   - ☐ **a.** tall stalk.
   - ☐ **b.** large leaf.
   - ☐ **c.** thick root part.

2. To find an edible plant, you need to know where the plant grows and
   - ☐ **a.** how it tastes.
   - ☐ **b.** what it looks like.
   - ☐ **c.** how it is cooked.

3. Because of the bitter tannin in acorns, you should
   - ☐ **a.** never eat them.
   - ☐ **b.** handle them carefully.
   - ☐ **c.** soak or boil them before eating.

4. A person living in the wild who knew about edible plants would probably
   - ☐ **a.** go hungry.
   - ☐ **b.** have many plants to eat all year.
   - ☐ **c.** have few plants to eat in only one season of the year.

5. From the article, you can conclude that a meal of wild plants
   - ☐ **a.** is dangerous.
   - ☐ **b.** is not possible.
   - ☐ **c.** is possible if you know what to look for.

C. Reading Strategies

1. Recognizing Words in Context

Find the word *poisonous* in the article. One definition below is closest to the meaning of that word. One definition has the opposite or nearly the opposite meaning. The remaining definition has a meaning that has nothing to do with the other two words. Label the definitions **C** for *closest*, **O** for *opposite* or *nearly opposite*, and **U** for *unrelated*.

_____ **a.** helpful

_____ **b.** grateful

_____ **c.** harmful

2. Distinguishing Fact from Opinion

Two of the statements below present *facts*, which can be proved. The other statement is an *opinion*, which expresses someone's thoughts or beliefs. Label the statements **F** for *fact* and **O** for *opinion*.

_____ **a.** Acorns are the nuts of oak trees.

_____ **b.** Gooseberries taste better than strawberries.

_____ **c.** Poisonous plants may look like edible plants.

3. Making Correct Inferences

Two of the statements below are correct *inferences*, or reasonable guesses, that are based on information in the article. The other statement is an incorrect, or faulty, inference. Label the statements **C** for *correct* inference and **I** for *incorrect* inference.

_____ **a.** Watercress is more similar to spinach than it is to potatoes.

_____ **b.** You might trip over arrowhead roots as you walk next to a river.

_____ **c.** If you see a shrub with leaves shaped like hands, it could be a gooseberry shrub.

4. Understanding Main Ideas

One of the statements below expresses the main idea of the article. Another statement is too general, or too broad. The other explains only part of the article; it is too narrow. Label the statements **M** for *main idea*, **B** for *too broad*, and **N** for *too narrow*.

_____ **a.** Many wild plants are edible.

_____ **b.** Although many wild plants have edible parts, people must be able to tell which plants are safe before eating them.

_____ **c.** People can use acorns to make flour, but first they need to extract the bitter tannin.

5. Responding to the Article

Complete the following sentences in your own words:

One of the things I did best while reading "A Meal of Wild Forest Plants" was

_____

I think that I did this well because _____

D. Expanding Vocabulary

Content-Area Words

Complete each analogy with a word from the box. Write in the missing word.

clover	tubers	acorns	bitter	thorns

1. roots : carrots :: _____ : potatoes

2. cotton : soft :: _____ : sharp

3. oranges : fruit :: _____ : nut

4. dog : animal :: _____ : plant

5. sweet : sugar :: _____ : tannin

Academic English

In the article "A Meal of Wild Forest Plants," you learned that *extract* means "to take something out of something else." *Extract* can refer to separation of chemicals. *Extract* can also mean "to draw out something with effort," as in the following sentence.

It is wrong to extract a false confession.

Complete the sentence below.

1. The firefighters worked to *extract* the child from _____

Now use the word *extract* in a sentence of your own.

2. _____

_____

You also learned that *expert* is a noun that means "someone who knows a great deal about a subject." *Expert* can also be an adjective that means "showing a great deal of knowledge about a subject," as in the following sentence.

An expert gardener has many gardening tools.

Complete the sentence below.

3. He became quite *expert* at cooking by spending a lot of time in _____

Now use the word *expert* in two sentences of your own.

4. _____

5. _____

 Share your new sentences with a partner.

Before You Read

 Think about what you know. Read the title and first paragraph of the article on the opposite page. What do you predict the article will be about? What do you know about how we hear the sounds around us?

Vocabulary

The content-area and academic English words below appear in "What Is Sound?" Read the definitions and the example sentences.

Content-Area Words

acoustic (ə kōos′tik) related to hearing or sound
Example: Theaters must have good *acoustic* quality so that audiences can hear well.

vibrations (vī brā′shənz) shaking movements that go back and forth or up and down
Example: You can see the *vibrations* of a guitar string when you pluck it.

pitch (pich) the highness or lowness of a sound
Example: The *pitch* of a scream is very high.

eardrum (ēr′drum′) a thin layer of skin that separates the parts of the ear
Example: The *eardrum* vibrates when sound waves enter the ear.

impulses (im′puls iz) signals that travel in waves
Example: Nerve *impulses* carry messages about sound from the ear to the brain.

Academic English

detect (di tekt′) to discover or notice
Example: The human ear can *detect* different sounds.

aware (ə wār′) knowing about something or that something is present
Example: The weather forecast makes people *aware* of weather conditions.

Do any of the words above seem related? Sort the seven vocabulary words into two or more categories. Write the words down on note cards or in a chart. Words may fit into more than one group. You may wish to work with a partner for this activity.

 Now skim the article and look for other words that are new to you. Write each new word and its definition in the Personal Dictionary.

While You Read

Tip! **Think about why you read.** Have you ever thought about how your ears help you hear sounds? Write a question about hearing that you would like to know the answer to. As you read, you may find the answer.

What Is Sound?

1   The human ear can **detect** many sounds. The low sound of a heavy object hitting the ground, the soft sound of a fan, and the loud ring of a bell are just a few of the different sounds that we can hear. If we want to understand why we can hear so many different sounds, first we need to know what sound is.

5   Sound is a type of energy that travels in waves. We call these waves sound waves, or **acoustic** waves. When an object moves, it may produce sound waves. As the object vibrates, or shakes, it causes tiny pieces of air called molecules to move as well. First it pushes the molecules together, and then it pulls them apart. This action makes a wave of sound that moves through the air. You can see the **vibrations** that
10   make sound waves when you pluck, or pull, the strings of a guitar. You can feel these vibrations if you place your fingers on your throat when you talk.

The speed of the vibration of an object sets the **pitch** of the sound that the object makes. A fast vibration makes short waves. Short waves make a sound that has a high pitch, such as the ring of a bell or the screech of car brakes. A slow
15   vibration makes long waves. Long waves make a sound with a low pitch, such as the growl of an animal or the hum of a refrigerator.

The strength of the vibration of the object determines how loud a sound is. A strong vibration makes big waves, and a weak vibration makes small waves. When you gently pluck a guitar string, the string vibrates weakly, and the sound
20   is soft. When you pluck the string with great force, the vibration is strong, and the sound is loud. We can measure the loudness or softness of a sound in units called decibels.

Humans and many animals have ears that enable them to hear sound. The shape of the human ear helps the ear gather sound waves and send them through a tube
25   to the **eardrum.** As the waves pass through the eardrum, they cause it to vibrate. The body changes the vibrations—whether fast, slow, strong, or weak—into **impulses** that travel along nerves to the brain. The brain then helps us understand the sounds we are hearing.

Humans cannot hear all sounds. Only certain animals are **aware** of high-pitched
30   sounds called ultrasound. Bats, dolphins, and whales use ultrasound to find food. Because humans can hear so many sounds, it may be hard to believe that some sound waves produce sounds that we cannot hear.

LANGUAGE CONNECTION

The word *detect* may remind you of another word you have seen: *detective.* The job of a detective is to detect, or notice and find, things that might help the police solve cases. What is a smoke *detector*?

CONTENT CONNECTION

A quiet library has a noise level of about 20 decibels. A rock concert has a noise level of about 110 decibels. Do you think loud noises can harm our ears?

After You Read

A. Organizing Ideas

What makes sound? How do we hear it? Complete the sequence chart below. In each box, write down one step in the process of making and hearing sound. You may add boxes if you want to add information. The first box has been done for you.

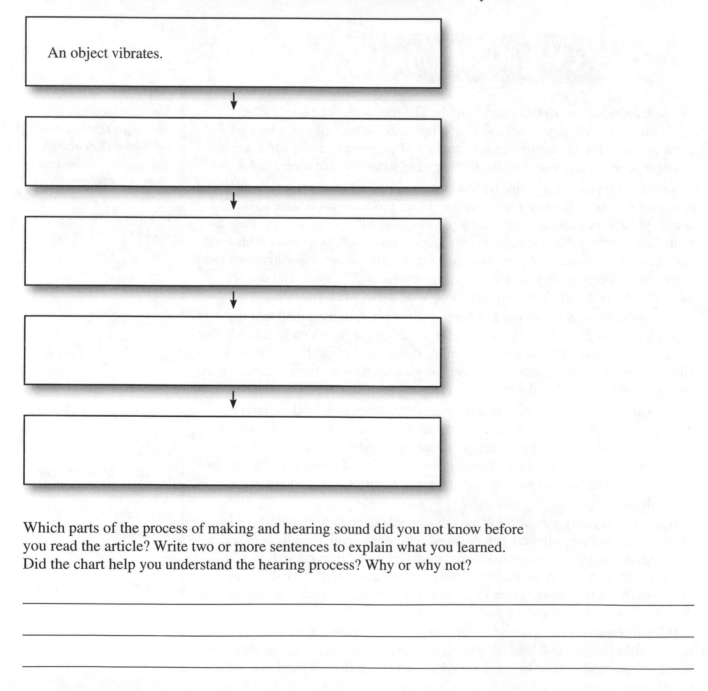

An object vibrates.

Which parts of the process of making and hearing sound did you not know before you read the article? Write two or more sentences to explain what you learned. Did the chart help you understand the hearing process? Why or why not?

_____

_____

_____

_____

B. Comprehension Skills

Tip! **Think about how to find answers.** Look back at different parts of the text. What facts help you figure out how to complete the sentences?

Mark box **a**, **b**, or **c** with an **X** before the choice that best completes each sentence.

Recalling Facts

1. Sound is a form of energy that travels in
   - ☐ **a.** waves.
   - ☐ **b.** routes.
   - ☐ **c.** packets.

2. The pitch of a sound is set by the
   - ☐ **a.** size of the noise.
   - ☐ **b.** distance to the ear.
   - ☐ **c.** vibration speed of an object.

3. The strength of the vibration that makes a sound determines
   - ☐ **a.** how loud the sound is.
   - ☐ **b.** how deep the sound is.
   - ☐ **c.** how fast the sound moves.

4. The unit that measures loudness is the
   - ☐ **a.** decibel.
   - ☐ **b.** amplifier.
   - ☐ **c.** wavelength.

5. A kind of high-pitched sound heard only by certain animals is
   - ☐ **a.** a scream.
   - ☐ **b.** ultrasound.
   - ☐ **c.** a radio wave.

Understanding Ideas

1. From the article, you can conclude that because outer space has no air, it has
   - ☐ **a.** no sound.
   - ☐ **b.** the same sounds as Earth.
   - ☐ **c.** certain animals that can hear sound.

2. Human beings hear
   - ☐ **a.** very few sounds.
   - ☐ **b.** every kind of sound.
   - ☐ **c.** many kinds of sounds.

3. We cannot hear sounds without
   - ☐ **a.** eyes.
   - ☐ **b.** earlobes.
   - ☐ **c.** an eardrum.

4. From the article, you can conclude that the high whistle of a teakettle is made up of
   - ☐ **a.** long waves.
   - ☐ **b.** short waves.
   - ☐ **c.** medium-length waves.

5. An electric guitar with the volume turned up would produce
   - ☐ **a.** no vibrations.
   - ☐ **b.** weak vibrations.
   - ☐ **c.** strong vibrations.

C. Reading Strategies

1. Recognizing Words in Context

Find the word *apart* in the article. One definition below is closest to the meaning of that word. One definition has the opposite or nearly the opposite meaning. The remaining definition has a meaning that has nothing to do with the other two words. Label the definitions **C** for *closest*, **O** for *opposite* or *nearly opposite*, and **U** for *unrelated*.

_____ **a.** close

_____ **b.** away

_____ **c.** dark

2. Distinguishing Fact from Opinion

Two of the statements below present *facts*, which can be proved. The other statement is an *opinion*, which expresses someone's thoughts or beliefs. Label the statements **F** for *fact* and **O** for *opinion*.

_____ **a.** Without ears, people and animals would not be able to hear.

_____ **b.** The sense of hearing is more important than the sense of sight.

_____ **c.** Our brains help us understand sounds.

3. Making Correct Inferences

Two of the statements below are correct *inferences*, or reasonable guesses, that are based on information in the article. The other statement is an incorrect, or faulty, inference. Label the statements **C** for *correct* inference and **I** for *incorrect* inference.

_____ **a.** The siren on a police car probably produces short sound waves.

_____ **b.** People would eat different types of food if they used ultrasound to find it.

_____ **c.** When you put your hand on your throat and sing, you feel vibrations that make sound waves.

4. Understanding Main Ideas

One of the statements below expresses the main idea of the article. Another statement is too general, or too broad. The other explains only part of the article; it is too narrow. Label the statements **M** for *main idea*, **B** for *too broad*, and **N** for *too narrow*.

_____ **a.** An object's vibrations produce sound waves that we use our ears and brains to hear and understand.

_____ **b.** Humans can hear many different sounds.

_____ **c.** A fast vibration forms short waves.

5. Responding to the Article

Complete the following sentence in your own words:

What interested me most in "What Is Sound?" was

_____

_____

D. Expanding Vocabulary

Content-Area Words

Complete each sentence with a word from the box. Write the missing word on the line.

acoustic	vibrations	pitch	eardrum	impulses

1. Sound waves and _____ waves are the same thing.

2. The high _____ of the whistle hurt my ears.

3. Our body changes vibrations into nerve _____ that travel to the brain.

4. Sound waves enter the ear and move through a tube to the _____.

5. When an object shakes, it causes _____ that make sound.

Academic English

In the article "What Is Sound?" you learned that *detect* means "to discover or notice."
Detect can describe the way people notice sounds. *Detect* can also describe the way
other things can be discovered or noticed, as in the following sentence.

   My sense of taste is very strong, so I can detect even a tiny amount of pepper in my food.

Complete the sentence below.

1. People use their noses to *detect* _____

Now use the word *detect* in a sentence of your own.

2. _____

   _____

You also learned that *aware* means "knowing about something or that something is
present." *Aware* can describe how certain animals know that food is near through
ultrasound. *Aware* can also describe how people know things, as in the following sentence.

   The students are aware that they will be taking a test tomorrow.

Complete the sentence below.

3. You become *aware* that you need food when you feel _____

Now use the word *aware* in two sentences of your own.

4. _____

5. _____

 Share your new sentences with a partner.

Climate and the Change of Seasons

Before You Read

 Think about what you know. Read the lesson title above. What do you know about the seasons that occur where you live? Do you know of a place where the seasons are different?

Vocabulary

The content-area and academic English words below appear in "Climate and the Change of Seasons." Read the definitions and the example sentences.

Content-Area Words

humid (hū′mid) moist or damp because of water in the air
Example: The *humid* air makes my clothes feel damp.

tropics (trop′iks) hot, sunny areas near the equator
Example: You would not need a winter coat if you lived in the *tropics*.

poles (pōlz) the north and south ends of Earth's axis
Example: The climate is very cold at Earth's *poles*.

season (sē′zən) one of four times of the year that have different weather conditions
Example: Summer is my favorite *season* because it is warm.

angle (ang′gəl) a shape formed by two lines that come from the same point
Example: You can bend your arm to form an *angle* at the elbow.

Academic English

contrast (kon′trast) a difference between two or more things
Example: I felt the *contrast* between the warmth inside and the cold outside.

occupy (ok′yə pī′) to live in or be in a place
Example: Many people *occupy* the neighborhoods in large cities.

Rate each vocabulary word according to the following scale. Write a number next to each content-area and academic English word.

4   I have never seen the word before.

3   I have seen the word but do not know what it means.

2   I know what the word means when I read it.

1   I use the word myself in speaking or writing.

 Now skim the article and look for other words that are new to you. Write each new word and its definition in the Personal Dictionary.

While You Read

 Think about why you read. Do you know why some places have different seasons? As you read, try to find the answer.

Climate and the Change of Seasons

1   Some parts of the United States have different weather during different times of the year. Cold and snowy winters may change to hot and **humid** summers. In other parts of the country, it is warm all year. In the **tropics,** near the equator, it is always hot. In **contrast,** it is always cold at Earth's **poles.** These places have
5   different climates, or usual weather patterns for an area. The most important reason for the different climates is the tilt, or slant, of Earth's axis as Earth orbits, or circles, the Sun.

Earth's axis is the imaginary line that goes through the middle of Earth. It goes from the North Pole to the South Pole. For half of the year, or half of Earth's orbit,
10   the northern half of Earth tilts toward the Sun. For the other half of the year, the southern half of Earth tilts toward the Sun. More direct light and heat reach the half of Earth that is tilted toward the Sun, so it is warmer on that half. On that half of Earth, the **season** is summer. The half of Earth that is tilted away from the Sun receives less direct heat and light. The season on that half of Earth is winter.
15   Summer starts in June in the northern half of the world, and summer starts in December in the southern half of the world.

The Sun's light shines on Earth in rays, or lines of light. These rays always form an **angle** with the surface of Earth. In the tropics along the equator, this angle does not change very much throughout the year. The tropics get direct sunlight all
20   year and are always hot. Instead of summer and winter, the tropics may have a dry season or a wet season, depending on how much rain falls.

The angle of the Sun's rays at the North and South Poles makes these places cold. In the summer, when a pole is tilted toward the Sun, it may get up to 24 hours of sunlight a day. However, the angle of the rays is very sharp. Because of
25   this, the heat of the rays is not very strong. In the winter, when the pole is tilted away from the Sun, the rays of the Sun hit the pole for only a few hours each day. During some winter days, the rays may not hit the pole at all. Winters at the poles are dark and very cold. Without the summer months in these and other cold regions, plants and animals probably could not survive. The length and warmth of
30   the summer in any particular region determine what kinds of plants and animals can **occupy** that region.

CONTENT CONNECTION

Earth takes one year to orbit the Sun. What else orbits the Sun?

LANGUAGE CONNECTION

The word *sharp* usually means "coming to a point," as in a sharp angle or a sharp pencil. It can also mean "extreme," as in a sharp change in direction. Can you use this meaning of *sharp* in a sentence?

After You Read

A. Organizing Ideas

What causes some places on Earth to have different seasons? In the space below, draw a picture of Earth and the Sun. Show the Sun's rays hitting part of Earth. Use the following labels in your drawing.

Sun	Summer	Axis
Sun Rays	Winter	North Pole
Earth	Equator	South Pole

What did you learn about why some places have different seasons? Write two or more sentences to summarize what you learned. How did the drawing help you understand the seasons? Explain your answer.

_____

_____

_____

_____

_____

B. Comprehension Skills

Tip! **Think about how to find answers.** Look back at what you read. The words in an answer are usually contained in a single sentence.

Mark box **a**, **b**, or **c** with an **X** before the choice that best completes each sentence.

Recalling Facts

1. The differences in Earth's climates and seasons are caused by
   □ **a.** the tilt of Earth as it orbits the Sun.
   □ **b.** the type of rays that come from the Sun.
   □ **c.** weaker rays as the Sun ages.

2. We call the imaginary line through Earth from the North Pole to the South Pole the
   □ **a.** axis.
   □ **b.** equator.
   □ **c.** pole line.

3. Strong light and heat warm the half of Earth that is
   □ **a.** facing the Moon.
   □ **b.** tilted toward the Sun.
   □ **c.** tilted away from the Sun.

4. The region that gets direct sunlight all year is the
   □ **a.** tropics.
   □ **b.** North Pole.
   □ **c.** South Pole.

5. The sharp angles between the Sun and the poles cause the poles to be
   □ **a.** hot all year.
   □ **b.** cold all year.
   □ **c.** hot in the summer and cold in the winter.

Understanding Ideas

1. In different regions of the world, seasons
   □ **a.** are different.
   □ **b.** are exactly alike.
   □ **c.** often do not exist.

2. An example of a place that has one period of complete darkness and one of constant daylight is
   □ **a.** the Sun.
   □ **b.** the tropics.
   □ **c.** the North Pole.

3. The season in the half of Earth that is tilted away from the Sun is
   □ **a.** summer.
   □ **b.** winter.
   □ **c.** the dry season.

4. From the article, you can conclude that when the northern half of Earth is tilted toward the Sun, the southern half is
   □ **a.** straight up and down.
   □ **b.** tilted away from the Sun.
   □ **c.** also tilted toward the Sun.

5. You can also conclude that when it is summer in the northern half of Earth, the season in the southern half is
   □ **a.** winter.
   □ **b.** also summer.
   □ **c.** the wet season.

C. Reading Strategies

1. Recognizing Words in Context

Find the word *imaginary* in the article. One definition below is closest to the meaning of that word. One definition has the opposite or nearly the opposite meaning. The remaining definition has a meaning that has nothing to do with the other two words. Label the definitions **C** for *closest,* **O** for *opposite* or *nearly opposite,* and **U** for *unrelated.*

_____ **a.** unreal

_____ **b.** bright

_____ **c.** real

2. Distinguishing Fact from Opinion

Two of the statements below present *facts,* which can be proved. The other statement is an *opinion,* which expresses someone's thoughts or beliefs. Label the statements **F** for *fact* and **O** for *opinion.*

_____ **a.** It would be better to live in the tropics than at the North Pole.

_____ **b.** The angle of the Sun's rays causes the South Pole to be cold.

_____ **c.** When one half of Earth is tilted toward the Sun, it is summer there.

3. Making Correct Inferences

Two of the statements below are correct *inferences,* or reasonable guesses, that are based on information in the article. The other statement is an incorrect, or faulty, inference. Label the statements **C** for *correct* inference and **I** for *incorrect* inference.

_____ **a.** It probably does not snow in the tropics.

_____ **b.** Different parts of the world have different plants and animals because of their climates.

_____ **c.** The climate of the South Pole is tropical during the summer months.

4. Understanding Main Ideas

One of the statements below expresses the main idea of the article. Another statement is too general, or too broad. The other explains only part of the article; it is too narrow. Label the statements **M** for *main idea,* **B** for *too broad,* and **N** for *too narrow.*

_____ **a.** The amount of rain is the main seasonal change in the tropics.

_____ **b.** The different climates and seasons around the world occur because of the way Earth tilts as it moves around the Sun.

_____ **c.** There are many different climates and types of seasons on Earth.

5. Responding to the Article

Complete the following sentence in your own words:

One thing in "Climate and the Change of Seasons" that I cannot understand is

_____

_____

D. Expanding Vocabulary

Content-Area Words

Cross out one word or phrase in each row that is not related to the word in dark type.

1. humid	damp	water vapor	desert	summer
2. tropics	sunlight	visible	equator	warm
3. poles	cold	North	East	South
4. season	four	winter	spring	October
5. angle	direction	shape	points	map

Academic English

In the article "Climate and the Change of Seasons," you learned that *contrast* is a noun that means "a difference between two or more things." *Contrast* can refer to differences in climate. *Contrast* can also refer to other differences, as in the following sentence.

The contrast between my older brother's and my heights is great.

Complete the sentence below.

1. The weather today, in *contrast* with the warmth of yesterday, is_____

Now use the word *contrast* in a sentence of your own.

2. _____

_____

You also learned that *occupy* means "to live in or be in a place." *Occupy* can also mean "to take up time or attention," as in the following sentence.

Writing my book report will occupy several hours of my time.

Complete the sentence below.

3. Children often *occupy* themselves by playing with _____

Now use the word *occupy* in two sentences of your own.

4. _____

5. _____

 Share your new sentences with a partner.

Writing an E-mail

Read the e-mail. Then complete the sentences. Use words from the Word Bank.

Word Bank

equipment   vehicles
strategy   contrast
aware

INSTA-CHAT

Dear Marc,

I had my first football practice today. Wow! In (1)_____ to easier

sports I have played, this sport is hard! The (2)_____ I wear is heavy,

but I am glad to have it. I was not (3)_____ that people would push

me and try to knock me down, but I won't give up. My (4)_____ is to

practice an extra hour each day and lift weights to strengthen my muscles.

Sports are great (5)_____ for energy, aren't they? Come on over this

weekend to help me practice!

Miguel

Reading a Journal Entry

Read the journal entry. Circle the word that completes each sentence.

Dear Journal,

When my parents asked me to help work in the garden, I thought
it would be boring. I was wrong! I have become an (**angle, expert**)
gardener! We grow different plants each (**season, clover**) as the
weather changes. I especially like roses—but not their (**vibrations,
thorns**).

Mom showed me how to (**extract, disturb**) and use color from
flowers to dye cloth. I pick flowers with lots of petals to (**pitch,
ensure**) that the color is bright.

Jin

 **Making Connections**

Work with a partner. Talk about what the words mean. How can you use the words to talk about nature? In the columns below, write each word, explain how it relates to nature, and describe what it makes you think of.

pressure	endangered	detect	predators	linked
acorns	humid	tropics	poles	occupy

Word	How It Relates to Nature	What It Makes Me Think Of

Use all of the words above in a paragraph of your own. Each sentence may include one or more of the words. To help you start writing, look at the ideas you wrote about. After you write your sentences, read them over. If you find a mistake, correct it.

Glossary

A

abdomen (ab′də mən) the main part of the body that contains organs in the middle region [7]

*__accumulate__ (ə kū′myə lāt′) to build up or increase in amount [10]

acorns (ā′kôrnz) nuts that grow on oak trees and are partly covered by a woody cup [18]

acoustic (ə kōōs′tik) related to hearing or sound [19]

*__adapt__ (ə dapt′) to change in order to become used to different conditions [2]

*__aid__ (ād) to provide help [3]

air pressure (âr presh′ər) the force caused by the weight of air [5]

amber (am′bər) clear yellow or brown hard material formed from the sap of pine trees [4]

angle (ang′gəl) a shape formed by two lines that come from the same point [20]

armored (är′mərd) protected by a covering that is often thick and made of metal [16]

astronomers (əs tron′ə mərz) people who study the science of the planets and stars [1]

*__aware__ (ə wâr′) knowing about something or that something is present [19]

B

bathyscaphes (bath′i skāfs′) armored ships, with space inside for people and equipment, that explore deep underwater [16]

bitter (bit′ər) having a sharp, unpleasant taste [18]

C

*__challenge__ (chal′inj) something that is difficult to do [11]

*__chemicals__ (kem′i kəlz) substances that cause and experience changes [3]

claw (klô) sharp, curved object that can hold or grab something [13]

climate (klī′mit) weather conditions in a certain area over time [3]

clover (klō′vər) plants that have small green leaves that have three or four parts [18]

companies (kum′pə nēz) groups of people who work or do business together [15]

compost (kom′pōst) a mixture of dead plants and food waste that makes soil healthy [15]

*__compound__ (kom′pound′) made of more than one part [13]

*__comprises__ (kəm prīz′əz) is made of or includes [1]

concentrated (kon′sən trāt′əd) grouped in one place [17]

continuous (kən tin′ū əs) not stopping [4]

*__contrast__ (kon′trast) a difference between two or more things [20]

control panels (kən trōl′ pan′əlz) areas with buttons and dials that control a machine [8]

current (kur′ənt) streams of air, water, or electricity that flow in a certain direction [4]

cycle (sī′kəl) a series of steps that repeat themselves regularly [9]

D

damage (dam′ij) harm or injury that causes something to be broken or useless [5]

deposits (di poz′its) materials that are left behind, often at the end of a river or stream [10]

destroyed (di stroid′) ruined or killed [6]

*__detect__ (di tekt′) to discover or notice [19]

*__device__ (di vīs′) a machine or tool created for a certain purpose [4]

directions (di rek′shənz) lines that something moves, faces, or lies along [14]

discovery (dis kuv′ər ē) something new that has not been known or found before [4]

*__dispose__ (dis pōz′) to get rid (of); to throw away [15]

disturbs (dis turbz′) bothers; changes the way something normally is [17]

dreaming (drēm′ing) thinking, feeling, or seeing pictures while asleep [9]

*__duration__ (doo rā′shən) the amount of time something lasts [5]

E

eardrum (ēr′drum′) a thin layer of skin that separates the parts of the ear [19]

ecosystem (ē′kō sis′təm) plants and animals that live together in an area of nature [6]

enclosed (en klōzd′) surrounded on all sides [12]

*__encounter__ (en koun′tər) to meet or come across something [7]

endangered (en dān′jərd) in danger of dying out or disappearing [17]

*__ensure__ (en shoor′) to make sure [17]

environment (en vī′rən mənt) the surroundings of a plant or animal that affect its life [11]

---

environmental (en vī´rən ment´əl) relating to the world around a plant or an animal [17]

equator (i kwā´tər) an imaginary line that cuts Earth into a top half and a bottom half [5]

equipment (i kwip´mənt) anything needed for someone to do something [16]

erosion (i rō´zhən) the slow wearing away of soil and rock, caused by water or wind [6]

*****error** (er´ər) a mistake [12]

*****eventually** (i ven´choo ə lē) at a later time [11]

experiment (iks per´ə mənt) a test used to discover or learn something [14]

*****expert** (eks´purt) someone who knows a great deal about a subject [18]

exposed (iks pōzd´) allowed to have light shine on it [12]

*****extract** (iks trakt´) to take something out of something else [18]

F

*****features** (fē´chərz) parts of the body that people see or notice [7]

fertile (furt´əl) able to produce crops or plants easily and plentifully [6]

fertilize (furt´əl īz´) to add nutrients, such as minerals, to the soil to help plants grow [15]

flooding (flud´ing) the rising or overflowing of water over land [5]

focuses (fō´kəs iz) aims something at a certain point [2]

formations (fôr mā´shənz) shapes composed of rock or mineral deposits [10]

fragrances (frā´grəns iz) sweet or pleasing smells [3]

fusion (fū´zhən) the process of using great heat to combine elements [1]

G

gears (gērz) wheels connected at the edges with teeth [13]

glowing (glō´ing) shining; letting off light and sometimes heat [1]

government (guv´ərn mənt) people that control a place, such as a city, state, or country [6]

gravity (grav´ə tē) the force that pulls objects toward a star or planet, such as Earth [1]

H

helmet (hel´mit) a cover or hat that protects the head by surrounding at least part of it [16]

humid (hū´mid) moist or damp because of water in the air [20]

I

illnesses (il´nis iz) diseases or sicknesses [3]

*****images** (im´ij əz) the mind's pictures of things [2]

impulses (im´puls iz) signals that travel in waves [19]

inclined plane (in klīnd´ plān) a flat, tilted surface [13]

instant (in´stənt) ready very quickly [12]

*****intense** (in tens´) very strong [5]

J

joints (joints) places where two bones meet or join, such as a knee or an elbow [7]

L

laboratories (lab´rə tôr´ēz) places where scientific experiments or tests are done [3]

*****linked** (lingkt) connected [16]

M

matter (mat´ər) anything that takes up space and can be weighed [4]

mission (mish´ən) a specific job that a person or group must do [8]

mission control (mish´ən kən trōl´) the people on Earth who talk with and help astronauts in space [8]

moody (moo´dē) having emotions, or feelings, that change often [9]

muscles (mus´əlz) tissues in the body that work together to move parts of the body [2]

N

nerve (nurv) a tiny, ropelike band of tissue that carries signals between the brain, spinal cord, and other parts of the body [2]

O

*****occupy** (ok´yə pī´) to live in or be in a place [20]

*****ongoing** (on´gō´ing) continuing; not stopping [10]

organ (ôr´gən) a part of the body that does a specific task or job [2]

P

pigment (pig´mənt) something that gives color [2]

pincers (pin´sərz) claws used for grabbing and holding [7]

---

* Academic English word   Lesson numbers appear in brackets.

pitch (pich) the highness or lowness of a sound [19]

poisonous (poi′zə nəs) full of poison, a substance that may cause sickness or death [15]

poles (pōlz) the north and south ends of Earth's axis [20]

pollution (pə lōō′shən) garbage or unhealthy chemicals in the air, water, or soil [15]

*__portion__ (pôr′shən) one part of a whole [4]

predators (pred′ə tərz) animals that hunt and eat other animals [17]

pressure (presh′ər) force that presses down from one thing onto another [16]

prey (prā) an animal that is hunted or killed for food [7]

projects (prə jekts′) causes a shadow, light, or image to appear on a surface [12]

properties (prop′ər tēz) special features of something [14]

protein (prō′tēn) a material in all living cells that people need for health [7]

R

receding (ri sēd′ing) moving back or away [11]

record (ri kôrd′) to set down on paper [12]

recover (ri kuv′ər) to get back to a normal state [9]

recruits (ri krōōts′) new members of a group or team [8]

*__regions__ (rē′jənz) parts or areas of something [6]

*__relaxed__ (ri lakst′) at rest rather than tense or worried [9]

remains (ri mānz′) materials that are left over, usually after a living thing dies [10]

*__restore__ (ri stôr′) to put something back the way it was before [6]

*__reversed__ (ri vurst′) changed to the opposite [12]

rotting (rot′ing) the decaying or spoiling of a once-living thing [3]

S

seashore (sē′shôr′) land near or on the edge of the sea [11]

season (sē′zən) one of four times of the year that have different weather conditions [20]

*__sequence__ (sē′kwəns) the order things are in [14]

shovel (shuv′əl) a tool with a blade and a long handle that can be used to pick up and move dirt [13]

*__simulate__ (sim′yə lāt′) to feel or look like something else [8]

*__site__ (sīt) the place where something is [15]

spectrum (spek′trəm) the series of colors that white light separates into [14]

stages (stāj′iz) lengths of time or steps in a process [9]

stalactites (stə lak′tīts) long rocks that hang from the ceiling of a cave [10]

stalagmites (stə lag′mīts) long rocks that rise from the floor of a cave [10]

*__strategy__ (strat′ə jē) a plan for how to get something done [17]

suction cup (suk′shən kup) a cup-shaped object that sticks to a flat surface through lowered air pressure [11]

*__survive__ (sər vīv′) to remain alive [1]

systems (sis′təmz) groups of parts that work together [13]

T

*__task__ (task) a job or piece of work [13]

*__theory__ (thē′ər ē) an unproved explanation based on known facts [9]

thorns (thôrnz) short, sharp points on the stem or branches of a plant [18]

tides (tīdz) the rise and fall of water levels that, in most oceans, takes place twice each day [11]

tropics (trop′iks) hot, sunny areas near the equator [20]

tubers (tōō′bərz) large, fleshy parts of underground roots that store food for a plant [18]

U

*__undergo__ (un′dər gō′) to go through or experience something [8]

universe (ū′nə vurs′) everything that exists in space, including stars and planets [1]

V

*__vehicles__ (vē′ə kəlz) machines that move people or things from one place to another [16]

vibrations (vī brā′shənz) shaking movements that go back and forth or up and down [19]

*__visible__ (viz′ə bəl) able to be seen [14]

W

wavelength (wāv′lengkth′) the distance between two high points of a wave [14]

waves (wāvz) moving ridges, such as those on the surface of water [5]

weightlessness (wāt′lis nis) the feeling of having little or no weight [8]

---

* Academic English word

Lesson numbers appear in brackets.

Personal Dictionary